How to Live
When You Want to Die

ANDY HULL

6'1"   LH PITCHER
175 LBS.   SWITCH HITTER

How to Live
When You Want to Die

By
LeAnn Hull

Printed in the United States of America

ISBN 978-1692982652

You Matter Books, LLC
PO Box 75067
Phoenix, AZ 85087
www.leannhull.com

DEDICATION

This book is dedicated to our son, Andy, who brought
sunshine to all who knew him. His sunshine helped us
survive in the midst of the darkest days of our lives.
Andy's love and passion for life will continue propelling
us forward until that glorious day when we are all
reunited in Heaven.

Never give in, never, never, never, never—
in nothing, great or small, large or petty—
never give in except to convictions
of honor and good sense.

— Winston Churchill

Writing this book began as a way for me to honor my son, Andy, and his memory. As I got further into the process of writing and time passed, more and more kids had also died by suicide in my home state of Arizona. Reaching out to the other Moms shortly after their kids transitioned to Heaven became another mission of mine. I felt strongly that only another Mom could reassure them that it was possible to move forward with their lives.

Each of the images that appear in between the chapters is a drawing from a Mom to her child, and those children are sharing space in Heaven with my Andy. Please take a moment to say their names and send out a prayer of light and love to the family left behind.

Thank you.   LH

FOREWORD
by Clay Hull

My name is Clay, but in our family, I've had many names. I am LeAnn's husband Clayty, to Michael I'm Daddio, Beth has always called me Dad, Joshua called me Pedro, and Andy (he was always Andrew to me), always called me Father. I've treasured my relationships with each of them and still do, as well as each title bestowed.

One memorable afternoon, LeAnn called as I was heading home from work. "Clay, I want you to write the foreword to my book." The tears fell like a Southeast Texas rainstorm, my eyes blurred, and I stammered some sort of response as I pulled off at the very next exit. *I can't write!* I thought to myself as I sobbed, but my desire to share the LeAnn Hull, the "Mama Hull" that I love so dearly with as many people as I can ruled the day.

For me, this has been sort of an audio book. From time to time, LeAnn would read sections and chapters to me as this book developed. Her words and feelings captured me every time. LeAnn is a gifted communicator. She has taken her sorrow and brokenness and molded a message that will make you cry, then make you laugh. What you won't hear her do, though, is tell you how she supported our whole family. She is modest when she tells of the hundreds of Andrew's friends who looked to her for strength and understanding after Andrew moved on. She doesn't tell you that she never pushed us or belittled us for being on a different journey than hers. And you won't hear her say how many times she has taken middle-of-the-night calls or driven hundreds of miles to console a devasted mom or dad.

This book will take you on a journey of twists and turns and also hit highs and lows. LeAnn will share stories of the many friends and acquaintances who knew Andrew and the love he shared with them. The stories of Andrew's impact on others will no doubt amaze you, as much as they shocked us. Andrew touched and changed more people in his 16 years than most who live full lives well into their eighties and beyond. There are many vignettes – too numerous to mention here – of how the yellow "You Matter!" bracelets have been put in the right hand at just the right time to light a candle of hope for a stranger who has been lost.

Woven into every chapter are hard truths and real coping tools that you can draw from to support your own loss or the loss of others. LeAnn doesn't sugar coat her message. Yet, she offers a positive role model and encouraging thoughts that I believe are a blessing bestowed on her so that she can shower you, in your path forward, with understanding of the strength and control you can have over your grief, if you wish.

LeAnn and I have been married almost 40 years now, and together for several more. From the start, we made a conscious decision to not let life and its unknowns shake our resolve to remain the best of friends and be good parents, no matter what. Our faith in God and love for others has given us opportunities to discover who we are in good times, but even more so when times are tough.

Whoever you are and wherever you are in this journey, there is support available for you and, more importantly, there are no doubt people who believe "You Matter!" As you read this book, may the words that were Divinely delivered through LeAnn transform your life, and give you hope and resolve to move forward with whatever challenges you may be facing.

ACKNOWLEDGMENTS

This book exists, first and foremost, because of the Divine direction I received following one of the most significant and tragic events of my life. While I know that God was present with me before, nothing compares to the direct spiritual influence that has been guiding my every move and thought since December 11, 2012. The passion to write this book consumed me and the words that flew onto the pages came with a strong sense of urgency, as well as very clear direction. Needing to bare my soul for the sake of others also experiencing trauma superseded all the pain I felt during this writing process, when reliving the first eighteen months after Andy moved to Heaven.

To my husband, Clay, who has been my biggest cheerleader, confidant and lover; there aren't sufficient words to describe your unwavering support both, emotionally and financially, of me throughout our marriage – but all the more so since Andy moved. Thank you for believing in me no matter what and being steadfast in your support of me and my dreams. No other person on the planet will ever share this space of losing our Andy in the way that we do. My undying gratitude and love are forever yours.

To my daughter, Beth, who helped lift me up off of the concrete, both physically and spiritually, moments after our devasting news. Thank you for tucking me into bed that first night and painting the blue heart over the red stain of Andy's life that had been left on his bedroom floor. I am forever grateful for your tender love and daily connection in my life.

To my son, Michael, who needed me to help him through his brokenness. This new sense of life-saving purpose propelled me past my own pain, thus allowing me more time to heal. As you have regained your footing, your focus has now been shifted to my well-being, which is such an unexpected but wonderful blessing. Watching you grow through your pain has given me renewed hope and strength. Thank you for not giving up on your life. I need you.

To my son, Josh, who was such a strong support in the beginning but has now disappeared from all of our lives. I miss hearing you call me "Momma." I miss your arms wrapped around me with your big hugs. I miss you. I will never leave you and will wait with an open heart and outstretched arms for the day that you return to our family. I love you forever.

To my grandchildren, Gavin, Lilly and Raiden, who gave me a reason to live. You are my future hope for the possibility of more healing. Wanting to be a whole and happy Grandma for you gave me the drive to put the pieces of my heart and life back together after Uncle Andy moved. I choose joy and love for the three of you and for me. It is a decision to not just survive, but to thrive.

To my "firefighter friends," Craig, Laura, Michelle and Cindy, who rushed into the flames of devastation without hesitation. You came and you stayed. Without you walking beside me on this rough and rocky road, I'm not sure if the story would look as beautiful as it does now. Your comfort, compassion and love endured through the darkest of times. You never let me go, even when I could no longer hold on. Thank you for loving my Andy and me so unselfishly.

To my new "shining light sisters," Carol and Elizabeth, who share with me the common bond of the physical loss of a child. Our endless early morning coffees and afternoon cocktails have been a refuge for my soul and heart. We are bound together by a collateral beauty that is deeper than family blood. We are mothers of sons across the veil and are filled with the spiritual knowledge of life after life. The two of you have opened my eyes to a greater possibility for my life here and later. Thank you for the surprise of our sisterhood.

To my Mom, Mary, who is in Heaven. I am forever grateful for the strong woman that you created me to be. You will forever be my role model and hero. With generosity and love,

I watched you give endlessly to me and my family. There is nothing you wouldn't have done for me, which I have tried to emulate for my children. Thank you for showing me how to believe in myself and to never, never, give up. Please look after my Andy.

To my editor, Mary Langford, who was brave enough to invest her heart and share this journey of loss, hope and love with me. Our connection was instantaneous and has only deepened the further we got into this editing process. The more you became immersed in my Andy's "sunshine," the more evident your love for him was. I'm thrilled that you "like to move it, move it" as much as he did. With two hearts as one we allowed the words to become this beautiful story and I thank you for your dedication and most importantly, your sacred heart.

Christina Tournant 6/24/1997 - 3/5/2015

Caring
Helpful
Radiant
Intelligent
Shining Light
Tender
Ineffable
Noteworthy
Athletic

We Will Continue Your Fight

Christina Tournant
1997-2015

1

NO ANSWER

On December 11, 2012, as my workday began winding down, I called my sixteen-year old son's cell phone to find out his schedule after baseball practice. It rang and rang and rang. No answer. Strange, as Andy always answered my calls, even when he was upset with me. Don't panic, I kept telling myself. Keep calm. Maybe he lost his phone or he's turned off the ringer. I was sure he would see that I was calling and buzz me right back.

But even as I was having this private conversation with myself, my stomach started feeling queasy and unsettled. It was that funny feeling you get in your gut when you sense that something isn't quite right. The longer I went without hearing from him, the worse things became. My heart began racing, and I felt some sense of impending doom. Life was in full swing for Andy and the other varsity baseball players, so clear communication between us was essential, and he knew it. We always talked several times each day.

I called Cameron, a buddy of his from school, to see if he had seen Andy, but when Cameron answered, he told me that he was just coming back from the University of Arizona where he had been visiting with the college baseball coaches. Cameron hadn't even gone to school that day and had no idea of Andy's whereabouts. Now slightly more panicked, I called another one of his friends, who told me that Andy had left school just after second hour that morning, around nine o'clock.

With this new piece of information, I was feeling full-fledged panic and horror, as it was now three o'clock, and it was six hours earlier that Andy had apparently walked off the campus grounds and disappeared into thin air. Andy rarely missed school, and he certainly never left school without a good reason.

I closed my computer at work and frantically headed out to my car while calling friend after friend after friend of my son, and their parents, too, to see if anyone had seen my Andy.

Earlier in the day, I had asked Craig, a friend of mine who was retired, to go to my house and meet some prospective housecleaners. I was fairly sure I wouldn't be able to leave work early enough to meet them myself, so he happily agreed to meet with them at my house that afternoon. As I was now practically running in the direction of my car, I called Craig to see if maybe Andy was there with him, at home. I called and called and called, but he didn't answer either.

All the way home, as I sped down the road to my house, a feeling of dread consumed me like I had never before experienced. After I'd exhausted the list of Andy's close friends that I had numbers for, I also called all of his coaches and anybody else I could think of who might have a clue as to Andy's whereabouts that afternoon.

What is it that instinctively warns us that something terrible has happened? Is it intuition? Is it God trying to prepare us for what awful things he knows lay ahead? Or is it just our bodies' chemistry kicking into action on overdrive?

As I turned the corner onto my little street and made my way toward my house, I saw the worst thing any parent could ever see—paramedics and fire trucks lined the street right in front of my home. Even now, many years after the fact, I can still picture that scene in my mind like it was yesterday.

I threw my car into park, flew open the car door, and ran toward my house screaming—but the first responders wouldn't let me anywhere near my house.

I yelled, "Where's my son?"

Out of the mouth of a deputy sheriff came deafening words I was never prepared to hear. "I'm so sorry, ma'am. He's dead."

I dropped onto the concrete.

2

PLAY BALL

It was a beautiful October morning in Arizona in 2012. At the Peoria Sports Complex near Phoenix, the grass was gleaming as morning dew blanketed the baseball field. We'd waited for this moment for what had seemed like a lifetime. Now, all the stars had finally aligned and were ready to guide us into the next phase of what had already been an unbelievably exciting baseball journey for my beautiful teenage son Andy.

It looked like a scene right out of a movie. The baseball scouts, college and pros alike, were lined up behind the backstop with their radar guns, waiting for all the prize athletes to take their places on top of the pitching mound. The Arizona Junior Fall Classic was a moment that all baseball players waited for each year with great anticipation, in hopes that they would be discovered and skyrocketed instantly into athletic stardom.

Back and forth I paced, out of sight, so as not to agitate our left-handed throwing machine. After all his years of hard work, practice, and determination, Andy was finally ready for takeoff. He had spent years playing up to ten games on many weekends and also major holidays in assorted tournaments. Even after the sun went down, he threw pitch after pitch to his pitching coach, strengthening not just his arm, but also his focus and concentration. When Andy wasn't throwing the ball, he spent time in the batting cage near our neighborhood hitting that tough-as-nails nine-inch white sphere over and over again.

At home, Andy and his buddies played endless hours of catch and practiced their various baseball tricks with each other. Who among them could spin and twist the bat best? Who could throw the ball up in the air and catch it behind their backs? Who could pitch the nastiest curve ball? The knuckleball was no contest. Andy had the deadliest one of all. Never did my son tire of this game.

After what seemed like an eternity, it was finally Andy's turn on the mound. The first batter had taken his place in the batter's box and was waiting to see what kind of arsenal that his opponent was about to deliver. As Andy's fingers searched for precisely the right position of the stitching, he prepared the ball behind him for his pitch. He glared at the eager batter without the slightest hint of any facial expression. Andy always knew what to throw and was absolutely certain of his success. He was only sixteen years old at the time, yet he was this perfect mixture of boy and man all wrapped up in his 6'0" tall, muscular body. He was such a beautiful specimen. And for someone his age, Andy had incredible control.

"Strike one... strike two... strike three. Out!" The first batter was eliminated before he ever realized what hit him. I knew instantly that Andy was in the zone and was no doubt going to deliver today. It was my beautiful son's day to shine.

Four innings later, I watched my man cub leap off the mound, literally, after retiring batter after batter after batter. Seven strikeouts, no hits, and no runs earned. Relief and immeasurable joy swept over me simultaneously, as I was certain that the phone would be ringing off the hook soon with many offers for this talented young man. He had performed exactly as we had all hoped, and his future was about to be handed to him on a silver glove.

As we left the ball field that day, Andy was distracted by a table of undisturbed virgin maple baseball bats that seemed to be calling his name. They were all lying there, in the wide open, enticing their potential new owners to bring them home. The noises that emanated from my son's throat as he caressed this plain piece of wood sounded like those of a grown man in the throes of passion.

"Please, Mom, I really need a new bat!" And as if to solidify the deal, the name on the bat he longed for was "The Nasty." I could tell how much it meant to Andy, and no doubt I wanted to give him the moon and the stars.

We walked away with a brand new $400 "investment" that came with a three-month warranty. Thank God, I thought, since it was not uncommon for bats owned by these powerhouse young ballplayers to split apart—not knowing, of course, that it wouldn't end up mattering how long that bat would last.

That bright, sunny day gave us no warning about the coming dark storm that would rip through and demolish our nearly perfect little world, shattering us and scattering us into the winds. It would take years for me to understand what caused it, develop skills for coping with the pain, and fully integrate what had happened into my life.

3

BIRTH ORDER

Andrew Daniel Mackenzie Hull was born on April 10, 1996, in a hospital room filled with many who were eagerly awaiting this glorious moment. His two brothers, one sister, grandmother, his dad and me (of course), and my best friend Kathy were all in attendance for this special occasion.

When the doctor first walked through the delivery room door, he exclaimed, "Holy smoke! I guess we should have ordered bleachers for all the fans of this much-anticipated baby!" Little did he know that this new tiny person would indeed be surrounded, all throughout his life, by many loving family and friends, literally cheering him on from the bleachers.

The arrival of our new baby was met, at first, with a great deal of apprehension on the part of his brothers and sister. Andy's siblings were a lot older and weren't quite sure how this new person might affect their already well-established birth order. Would this tiny baby throw all of their tidy lives into an uproar?

Andrew was our fourth child—and quite a surprise. He came as a blessing to my husband and me, since we were already well-seasoned parents, both in years and in experience. By the time young Andy came along, Clay and I had been married for sixteen years; a union that had already produced three other amazing gifts from God.

Our oldest son Michael was sixteen, always in charge, and had crowned himself our Golden Child. He was not only the family leader, he was the president of his student body in grade school and captain of his baseball team, too.

The second born, our daughter Bethany (Beth), was fourteen and totally excited about the process of my pregnancy and expected birth. Beth was such a comfort and helper to me all along, but especially as I began "nesting" in anticipation of the baby's birth, and as I walked up and down the halls of the hospital during labor. Beth was dubbed the Silver Child by the Golden one.

Last, but certainly not least, our youngest son Joshua (Josh) was eleven, and about to be dethroned as the baby of our tight-knit family. Or the Bronze Child, as he was called when Andrew came along in 1996. Or was he? Josh was actually given the prestigious Quintessential Freshman Award for all four years of high school, even though for three he was no longer a freshman. It was quite an exceptional honor, given to the person who most epitomized the awkward, goofy demeanor of a freshman. Even through all his genius, though, Josh had managed to maintain the family stature of "baby" throughout his youth.

As with many other new babies, there is a bit of a story behind the name of our fourth child. Are we going to name our little one after a beloved grandparent or ancestor? Will he or she be named in honor of Mom or Dad? How about something traditional, like John, Mary, Bill, or Jane? I know! Let's name our baby after some exotic fruit or color, like

Kiwi, Mango, or Fuchsia. I, personally, kind of like Mango. Just kidding.

While all of those names were great prospects, our problem was that everybody in the family had a different name picked out for our new arrival. I wondered, what should we do? Somehow, after a time, we managed to agree on three names, and thus was born Andrew Daniel Mackenzie Hull. Allowing the three "royalty" children to name the next in line to the throne eased some of the tension of possible displacement or disruption to their organizational family chart.

By this time, our family life had found a rhythm that was busy and comfortable. Our kids had evolved beyond the baby years and matured into the challenging, yet interesting, years of being teenagers. I'm sure that at some level, our kids were embarrassed that their mom was with child. How could that possibly happen? Lord knows, their parents didn't do stuff like that. I think that notion actually horrified them.

To be honest, the thought of starting all over again with diapers, nighttime feedings, and sleepless nights didn't exactly excite me either. In addition, how in the world would we balance all the activities our kids were involved with while tending to the ever-demanding needs of a brand-new newborn?

Since Clay is ten years older than I am, his reaction was even more interesting than mine. He was definitely not looking forward to adding to our financial burden for a minimum of another twenty years. His response to the news was quite unique. He spent the next nine months digging a pool in our back yard with a pick and shovel, having his own sort of timely labor, so to speak. I guess that's one way of handling stress.

It was easier becoming parents this time around than it had been the first go-round. We were calmer, more mature, better off financially, and the other kids were now older. In a way, it was almost as if we were raising an only child. In fact, I think that our older kids were sometimes jealous of Andy because he got some things that they were never privileged enough to get. But it wasn't like Andrew was our "favorite," or we liked the other kids any less. We just had more money and more time to do things now than we did before, when they were all little.

Every family has a birth order equipped with the natural feelings of who the Golden Child really is, and the consensus among all three of our older kids was that Andrew was our Platinum Child. It wasn't true, of course. As I said, it was simply economics and availability of time. However, truth is subjective and defined by each person's experiences and perceptions. As parents, we do our very best with and for each child we have, but the dynamics change as quantity and experience are added. Although we loved Andrew with all our hearts, Clay and I certainly did not love Andrew more than we love any of our three other children.

For the first several years, our little surprise bundle of joy was carried happily around to all of the other siblings' events. They were all very busy with their own various activities, and we didn't want to miss any part of our children's lives. Just about the time that one kid was getting a driver's license or going with a date to a first prom, Andrew was learning how to walk and also to talk. When we stepped back from the inherent chaos and took it all in, it was really quite comical.

As time went on, the tables began to reverse. The older kids soon became spectators of Andrew's life. I think they enjoyed rooting for him as much as we did, mainly because he was so loving and so darn funny. At an early age, like around five, Andy began doing impersonations, mimicking some of his favorite cartoon and movie characters. He especially loved to hop around and dance like the silly lemur in

Madagascar, to the beat of that film's trademark song, "I Like to Move It."

One day in the car, Andrew started talking about his "father in another place." Clay was driving at the time, and we gently corrected our little Andy, saying, "Your dad is driving the car, you silly boy!"

We were a bit miffed when Andy replied, "No, I'm talking about my father, not Dad." We didn't think all that much about it at that time, but since I've come to understand a lot more about the afterlife in the ensuing years, what Andy said that day makes a great deal of sense to me now. In that moment, I assumed he was talking about God, which he very well may have been. In time, I look forward to meeting Andy again in Heaven, where I will be able to ask him that question directly. No matter who he was talking to, though, I had no doubt he was talking about someone from another dimension.

Time continued to march on, and soon the older kids were heading off to college, the Air Force, and motherhood/nursing respectively. Meanwhile, back at home, Andrew became a lot like an only child because we had even more time and ease for devoting ourselves to him and all of his fun activities.

With the newly assigned roles of all of our kids, everything seemed in perfect order.

"Keep it real and just be yourself."

— David "D.J." Pelletier, Jr.
9/30/1994 - 4/12/2018

4

THE JOURNEY HOME

Screaming, screaming, screaming until my voice was completely gone and my body limp. I had the emptiest feeling inside, and yet I was consumed by the most excruciating pain I'd ever felt in my life.

There must be something innate that grabs ahold of the tiny spark within us that—no matter what comes our way—gives us the will to survive. All around me, everything became hazy and it seemed like I was an actor in a slow-motion movie. It was as if I was watching myself, from someplace outside myself, lying there on the concrete writhing in pain, in total disbelief and shock.

Thank God for that shock. In that space and time, our minds and bodies become instantaneously insulated; protected from further assault. So, we are able to function with some semblance of rational responses, even in that level of awful horror.

Huddled like a ball on the concrete and sobbing uncontrollably, I somehow managed to call my husband, Clay—who was working on location at an oil refinery in North Dakota—and almost screamed out the words "Andy's dead!"

Saying those words out loud to my dear husband was almost more painful than hearing them. I was working hard to validate information that my brain was still trying, with all its might, to make sense of and process. In total shock, Clay managed to eke out the words that he would be on the first flight home and would let me know when he'd be arriving, so I could pick him up at the Phoenix airport.

One by one, I managed to make the difficult calls to my mom and Andy's siblings, passing along news of the unbelievable horror that had just invaded our lives. Hearing myself say those dreaded words—"Andy's dead"—over and over, felt like I was having some sort of surreal out-of-body experience. I can't explain it any other way than that, as it seemed like a foreign someone had overtaken my voice, and I was listening to what was unfolding from some far-away place. Perhaps that is the mind's way of protecting itself, I'm not certain, but it sure felt otherworldly to me.

The only one of Andy's siblings I couldn't reach was Michael, the oldest, who at that time was in the Army, stationed on a boat somewhere in the Persian Gulf. The adept first responders, however, knew exactly how to begin the process of locating service men and women in case of emergencies. They reached out to the American Red Cross, which pretty quickly found Michael. They delivered the life-shattering news to him and arranged for his immediate transport back home. I still feel sick to my stomach when I imagine what that must have been like for Michael to receive such dreadful information when he was eight thousand miles away from home and his loved ones.

As humans, we naturally congregate together whenever tragedy strikes, so that we can support each other through it no matter how tough the situation may be. So, to be all alone and such a great distance away from his family must have been horrendous for my poor Michael. He has never ever spoken of it since Andy's death, but the mental condition that he arrived in two days later said everything. Without a doubt, Michael was broken and permanently damaged, maybe even more so than any of the rest of us, if that's even possible. Time would indeed show us the massive tornado that had destroyed Michael, and to a lesser degree, everyone who ever loved our Andy.

My calls had a ripple effect on other people's phones, as well. Whether by me, or by someone else—I don't remember—Andy's baseball coach was notified of his tragic suicide. Coach "Baum" Baumgartner immediately arranged a gathering of all the boys on all the high school teams, along with grief counselors and parents, for delivery of this very sad news. Eventually, all of Andy's friends and beloved teammates were notified, and we all began the long, lonely journey forward—without him.

As I lay annihilated on the concrete, arms and hands of strangers were trying to help pick me up off the ground. But all I could think was, why should I even get up? Isn't getting up the first sign of still living? This much I knew was true: I did not want to live any more, not even for one day, without my precious Andrew.

Somewhere in the midst of all the chaos, I was told by one of the first responders that my daughter, Beth, and her three little ones were inside the house. He said that we should all move to our next-door neighbors' house and begin making decisions about where we'd all spend the night. The detectives and county coroner would be busy processing the death scene in Andy's bedroom for quite some time. Inside that room, my son lay motionless from a self-inflicted gunshot wound to the head.

A couple of the first responders ushered me along to the home of our long-time neighbors, Thad and Florence Baird, who were trying their best to console me. Consumed by merciless grief, I sat down at their kitchen table and wondered if it was possible to will myself to stop breathing.

People began pouring into the Baird's home, sobbing and asking all kinds of difficult questions. Try as I might, I couldn't process what was going on at all. Well-intentioned friends proceeded to place in front of me glasses of wine, along with a number of Xanax and other similar types of sedatives, hoping to ease the unrelenting pain that now enveloped my mind and body.

Fortunately, I had not lost all my discerning abilities and that, alone, probably saved my life. I knew that even in the best of times, alcohol was a depressant and would not serve to make me feel any better in the long run. Why in the world would I want to drink something that would only add to my unending heartache and terrible state of mind? Lord knows, I could not have been any more depressed and devastated than how I was feeling at that moment in time. I also knew, on some level, that drinking might make taking my own life seem like a good idea.

I drew a deep breath, pushed aside all the wine and pills, and made my way down the hall to the bathroom. As I entered, I quickly shut the door behind me. For more than just a few moments, I gazed into the mirror in an attempt to reconcile, in my own reflection, that what was happening in that house that day was actually happening to me.

In that moment, I made two statements under my breath that, unbeknownst to me at the time, would pave the way for my future as I moved forward: I'm not the first mom to lose a child and I will praise You in the storm. Having been a Christian all my life, I realized in that moment that my faith had to be called into action if I was ever to survive this tragedy.

I wrapped my arms around myself tightly and, from the depths of my soul, screamed a silent scream as loudly as I possibly could. Time stood still, and for a moment I couldn't breathe, and then found myself gasping for air ... for life. Once I calmed a bit, I closed my eyes and gathered up the courage that had been huddling down deep inside me. I turned around and walked out the bathroom door to begin the long journey ahead of me.

Stunned and without any direction, all I could manage was to find my way back to a chair at the kitchen table. I watched in shock as Andy's friends and their parents passed by me, one by one, sobbing with such deep anguish, also in a state of shock. Never in a million years did any of us think that Andy Hull was capable of something like this. We never, ever thought that this happy, wonderful kid would leave our world in this way. For God's sake, Andrew's nickname was "Sunshine"—and, we had thought, aptly so.

Many hours later, a kind detective knocked on my neighbors' door to tell me that the medical examiner was now in our house, and we wouldn't be able to return home until his work there was complete. They suggested that we stay somewhere else for the night, perhaps with a family member or friend, or even in a nice hotel.

At that time, my daughter Beth and her three children (ages thirteen, eight, and six) were living with Clay and me, so finding a place large enough to accommodate all of us so last-minute was not going to be easy or preferable. So, I proceeded to tell the detective that we would be going home no matter what, and no matter how long we had to wait for them to finish up their respective duties. He made it clear that he thought it was a bad idea for us to go back into the house that night, but my gut told me otherwise, and I had to follow it. I knew it would be best for all of us.

After having spent seven exhausting hours at Thad and Florence's, we were finally allowed to return home around ten o'clock that night. As Beth and I walked tentatively, arm in arm, back to our house, we were half holding each other up to keep from collapsing. To my surprise, she asked me where I thought we would live now. Somewhere from deep within me, or maybe it was a voice I was hearing from Heaven, I knew that we were going to stay right here, right now, and continue making this home our home.

As we entered through the front door, right in the entryway hall, I was assaulted with an image that will remain etched in my mind forever: my beloved Andy in a body bag on a gurney. How I stayed upright is nothing short of a miracle. Maybe it was my deep desire to wrap my arms around my precious boy one more time that kept me standing. No mom should ever have to experience this type of horrific event.

As images of other moms who had lost a child swam through my head, I reminded myself that I wasn't the first mom to have lost her precious child. For some reason, that brought me comfort enough to hug my beautiful Andrew one last time. I told him "I love you forever" and let him go. Then, as they wheeled my life away on that gurney, I dragged the shell of a person that was left of me into my bedroom.

The detectives had told me not to go into Andy's room—which was directly across from mine and Clay's—until the restoration people had come and cleaned it up. I'm no masochist, so I followed their rules to a tee. Thank God, my daughter and her kids—my grandkids—were living on the other side of the house, which allowed them some respite from this awful reality.

Even though Beth was the daughter and I the mom, she assumed the role of caregiver for me that night, as well as many more nights to come. She tucked me in, and the darkness and emptiness in the house allowed me to sleep until four o'clock the next morning. I vaguely remember hearing the restoration people in Andy's room somewhere around midnight, but it wasn't enough to truly awaken me from my moment of fleeting peace. Apparently, Beth had stayed awake all night to keep watch over me and her kids, and to manage the cleaning people. She was my earthly angel.

Nighttime and sleep became my fast friends because it was only there that I could turn off my thinking and feeling. Everybody's process is different. Some people who experience grief like mine say they can't sleep, but not me. Sleep was my only reprieve; my only real respite from this terrible storm.

I can't begin to describe what that feeling of emotional and physical pain was like when I woke up the next morning and reality hit me smack in the face. I felt compelled to walk into Andy's room to verify that he was, in fact, really gone, so I did.

Much to my amazement, though, what I saw next was a selfless act of pure love. The restoration cleaning crew had torn out the carpet where Andy had laid, which exposed the underlying concrete. In the middle of that concrete section was painted a big, beautiful, deep-blue heart, about four feet wide.

As I stood there processing the scene, Beth walked into the room and wrapped her loving arms gently around me as she told me the story of the heart. She said that after the restoration crew left and she saw that the stain of blood had permeated through the carpet onto the concrete floor, she lovingly painted the blue heart over it. She did not want me to be faced with the unbearable image of my son's blood that had quickly soaked into the concrete.

How did she manage to do that for me? Being thirteen years older than her baby brother, Beth loved Andy like he was her child and her best friend, so the pain that she must have endured in order to save me from just a little bit more pain must have been tremendous. We both laid our limp bodies over the heart, Andy's heart, as we lay on the floor together and sobbed.

Later that same day, throngs of Andy's friends formed a steady stream of love into our home and hearts. They, too, must have needed proof for themselves that the horror they had experienced the night before was indeed reality. Besides confirmation, I believe they also were subconsciously looking for comfort and a roadmap for what lay ahead. How were they going to survive without Andy? He was their rock, their encourager. He was Sunshine.

I'm sure that it terrified Andy's friends to think that if he could do this, then who else? Their worlds had been forever shaken in just an instant. This event would become a defining moment for many, if not all, of them. Somewhere inside me, I knew that I was being given the opportunity to help, and to teach these kids how to process their own feelings of loss and grief. Ultimately, we all walked this journey together during the next several years, holding each other up emotionally and physically, too.

As each friend entered the house, they headed straight for Andy's room. I was surprised at their apparent lack of fear or inhibition about being in the same room where Andy had moved to Heaven in such a violent and sudden way. They seemed to need to be where he had been less than twenty-four hours before. As they gazed into Andy's room and noticed the big blue heart, everyone did the very thing that Beth and I had done earlier that morning; they laid their bodies across it and sobbed.

Some asked for permanent markers and began to write and draw all around the perimeter of the heart. They poured out their souls that day and offered Andy their love for all eternity. Some of them recounted with humor and fondness stories and adventures they had shared together with their wonderful compadre. Some wrote words about the future and vowed they would forever remember the special friend that my son had always been to them.

It didn't take long for me to realize that this was a great healing therapy for us all. We desperately needed and wanted to talk about Andy. We all wanted to tell our stories about how much this kid had impacted our lives. Everybody talked about Andy being their best friend, but how can one person be a best friend to so many? An enormous capacity for love had lived in Andy and would now continue on through the lives of all whom he had touched while here on this Earth plane.

Though I didn't realize it at first, I would come to learn so much about my son through the eyes and stories of his closest friends. Funny how you think you know someone well, only to learn that you had been privileged to see just a glimpse of the whole person he truly was.

Within forty-eight hours, all of our immediate family had arrived home. The earliest flight Clay could get out of North Dakota was the following afternoon. Kevin, a close friend of his in the oil industry, stayed all night and day with Clay until his flight was due to take off. Andy's brother Josh and his wife, Kristin, left their home on Minot Air Force Base almost immediately and drove all through the night, arriving in Phoenix nearly twenty-four hours later.

The last one to arrive was Michael, who had flown from some overseas base to his house in Seattle, Washington, where he and his wife, Soledad, boarded the first flight back to Phoenix the next day.

Clay's flight home from North Dakota was divinely appointed, as if all of the heavenly angels came down to Earth to escort a grieving dad home, where he'd say his final goodbyes to his son. One final glimpse of his cherished boy would be all my husband would get before all the moments he and

Andy had shared over his sixteen years would fade into precious memories.

The ticket agent made it known that Clay had snagged the last remaining seat on his flight to Phoenix. As Clay walked solemnly to his assigned seat and settled in for the long journey home, he noticed that the seat next to him was empty. While waiting for the missing passenger to arrive so the plane could take off, Clay's thoughts wandered back to fond memories of times spent with Andy. The pain he was feeling brought tears, and they flowed down his cheeks without his even caring whether anyone was watching.

Before long, the flight attendant announced that takeoff was imminent; yet the seat next to Clay was still empty. Weird, Clay thought, since the ticket agent had said that the flight was completely sold out. Plus, there was even a waiting list, so every single seat should have been occupied.

As the plane lifted off toward the heavens, Clay felt an overwhelming sense of calm and protection. No doubt the angels were at work soothing my husband's distraught soul. It was then that Clay felt Andy's presence in the seat beside him—the final seat on the plane—and Andy and his dad shared the rest of the ride home. This would be the first, but certainly not the last, of many visits from Heaven between father and son.

It was a reunion like no others. Clay, all the kids, and I would spend the next two weeks crawling through the mire and debris of not only the death of our son and brother, but death by suicide, and all of the shame and stigma that is packaged along with it.

5

THE DANCE

The next week was a complete blur of visitors offering heartfelt, yet painful, condolences. Looking back, it was probably harder on them than it was us because we were so numb from this massive trauma. We have all seen someone who has that empty stare and walks like a zombie. Well, that was us. I don't believe that it's humanly possible for anyone to really grasp what that brand of pain feels like until, God forbid, you experience it first-hand. Until that happens, our minds and bodies won't allow us to process that sort of pain on any deep or meaningful level. Perhaps it's a protective device that the Creator designed so that we don't unnecessarily experience anything that awful. Now that Andy's gone, I can see the true wisdom in this concept. I would never have wanted to understand this kind of pain before having lived through my own devastating loss.

How did we survive that next week, let alone all the weeks that followed? Shock. Plain and simple. I'm positive that shock is how we made it through those early days and weeks after Andy's passing. We somehow put one foot in front of the other and, baby step by baby step, made all the necessary plans and decisions that were facing us.

Every morning, my heart jolted awake and back into this new, horrific reality. It took nearly all that was left in me, but somehow, I would manage to get myself into the shower and I'd slowly, almost robotically, get ready for what lay ahead for me on that day. I had always taken great pride in my appearance, but the first year after Andy left, I didn't wear any makeup at all. In an odd sense, it was my own way of mourning my son. I didn't want people to look at me and tell me I looked nice since that would somehow, in my mind, mean that I was okay. I was not okay! Yes, I was functioning, but I would never, ever be the same.

Often, the doorbell would ring and people that I didn't even know would be standing on my front porch bearing food. Thankfully, most of them apparently didn't feel like talking. They just wanted to perform some act of service for our grieving family, which was just fine by me. Every meal or bag of groceries delivered spared my family from going to the supermarket where we might run into someone who'd want to offer up hugs and tell us how sorry they were for our loss. All we really wanted to do was crawl back into bed, duck our heads under the covers, and never wake up. If we never had to leave our house again, that would have been too soon.

I often think about all those kind-hearted people, friends and strangers alike, and wish I could thank everyone who so thoughtfully dropped off food, water, snacks, coffee, and even toilet paper. They unselfishly watered our plants, ran our errands, picked up the mail, or stayed with us at our house until we were finally able to fall asleep. Then they'd turn off the lights, lock the doors, and let themselves out. So many tender acts of love and service during those first few weeks allowed us to just "be."

Planning a memorial service for your child is the most unnatural thing for any human to have to suffer. Imagine looking back through photos and memorabilia of your family's life, and instead of laughing or smiling, you are struggling to decide if this is the one that should go in the slide show meant to best portray and honor the memories of your beloved child.

Karen, the mom of Colton—who was one of Andy's close friends—put together the most startling collage boards representing Andy's various achievements and adventures. She also created several stunning metal mannequins dressed in Andy's numerous hats and jerseys. Clay and I and the kids will always remember Karen's sensitivity for us and her caring heart during those first few difficult days. We're very grateful that she stepped up and took on this task and saved us the burden of recreating a life of one we so dearly loved who was gone from us way too soon.

Our two boys, Colton and Andy, had shared the last ten years together playing baseball, getting their trucks stuck in the mud, jumping off the roof into our backyard pool, and on and on with so many other wild and fun childhood antics. Interestingly, Karen wasn't a close friend of mine at the time Andy died, and shortly after the service, she ceased all contact with me. But for this one very challenging, horrible moment, she lifted this weight from me and carried it for our whole family. I will be forever grateful to Karen for her true acts of compassion and love.

Looking back, I'm amazed at how well my brain actually functioned and how clear some things were to me at that time. Without a doubt, I knew that it was up to me to carry on all the love for my beloved son. Andy's spirit would live on through me and all his other family members and friends. It was up to us to take him with us everywhere we went, and to not let the world forget Andy had lived.

The first step in that process was going to be his memorial service, and I felt strongly about how it should be conducted. I wanted the service to reflect Andy's nature; not just through the music we'd play, but through the stories I knew all of us would stand up and tell. No dress clothes for this event; it would be baseball jerseys or the awesome yellow smiley-face T-shirts that would later become a standard for the future Andy Hull's Sunshine Foundation. Even though there was no getting around the magnitude of this great loss, we didn't want this day to look as sad and somber as we all felt inside. Our Andy was always so full of life and sunshine, and we wanted everyone present to reflect this to the best of our abilities.

The day before the memorial, I went into Andy's large bedroom closet and pulled out a light blue jersey that had the words "Perfect Game" written in black across it. The year prior, Andy had played in a tournament bearing this exact title and had ironically pitched his first perfect game during that match. Slipping his jersey over my head, I at once felt connected to Andy. Breathing in his familiar essence, I felt cocooned and safe. For a brief moment, as I disappeared into the comfort of Andy's clothes, I was sheltered from the rest of the world.

Everyone was finally gathered together at home now, trying to make some sense of this unfathomable tragedy—but without much luck. Then, Monday, December 17, 2012, finally arrived. That morning, we dragged ourselves out to Andy's truck and the rest of our respective vehicles that would carry us all to the church where Andy's service would be held. We decided to forego the traditional caravan of limousines and town cars since we didn't want to define this awful moment any more than we actually had to. We tried to pretend to ourselves that this was just another ordinary day—even though we all knew that it wasn't.

Clay and I felt it only fitting to drive Andy's truck, formerly Clay's, a very well taken care of Ford F-150. It was such a proud part of our son's life. As my husband and I made our way over to the church, we both commented on what a beautiful crisp morning it was and how brightly the sun was shining. It was the perfect weather for our boy, our Sunshine Andy.

The location of Andy's memorial had to be changed at the last minute due to the extraordinarily large crowds that were expected to gather for his life's celebration. As it turned out, more than twenty-five hundred people showed up that day to pay their respects and say their final good-byes. How in the world did my son touch the lives of so many people in his short sixteen years of life? And how did I not know this until after he died?

As we walked through the entryway of the church, our senses were assaulted instantly by all of the colored memory boards and the metal mannequins that were proudly adorned with Andy's baseball jerseys and caps. With little exception, everyone who entered the vestibule that December morning did just as our family did—paused, reflected, and stepped back in time for this sacred viewing of a life gone way too soon.

Upon arrival, church officials had asked if we'd like to wait by ourselves in a private room until the service began. In unison, all of us said no, that we'd rather spend time reminiscing with Andy's friends.

Slowly, we parted ways and went off to greet—and be hugged by—the folks who meant the most to us and to Andy: His fellow ball players, Boy Scouts, faith friends, family, and various and sundry cohorts on a life that was so filled with adventure. Strangely, we somehow were able to maintain our composure through the constant barrage of I'm sorry's and other well-meant expressions of condolence.

After a time, I noticed that the rest of my family had already made their way to our row in the front of the church. As I listened to several of the songs Andy loved the most echoing throughout the sanctuary—from rock 'n' roll, to country, to contemporary Christian—I was beckoned by the familiar sounds to begin my long walk down the aisle. Glancing around, I caught—if only for a couple of brief moments—the many pained faces watching me make my way toward what felt like the end of my life.

It was surreal to look around the vast church and see all eyes fixed on me as I made my way down the seemingly endless aisle. Andy and I were always so close, and one would have had to be blind not to have noticed. I could feel their burning questions being shouted out through the sounds of silence piercing the church. How will she ever survive without Andy? Strangely, I felt compelled to assure them, through my demeanor, of my faith in God as well as my belief that I would indeed find a way through this deep menagerie of pain that now occupied my heart, as well as my soul. I would survive, even if only to honor the life of my precious son.

Finally, I reached the front row and took my place beside Clay and the only other people left who mattered to me in my life at that moment—my precious family. They would quickly become the glue that put my heart back together.

Sometime after the eclectic collection of music filled the church with Andy's most favorite songs, it was time for some uplifting messages from Scripture to be delivered to us from Andy's youth pastor. After Pastor Ken Sheets spoke, several of Andy's friends stood up on stage and told stories of their favorite adventures with our youngest son.

When the telling of tales finally ended, each of the boys, in unison, pulled out of their pockets a pair of Andy's boxers which—for some odd reason still unbeknownst to me—they all had. Then they simultaneously landed parallel back flips off the stage, as this was one of their band of brothers' most famous trademarks. Andy would have absolutely loved that. In fact, I'm certain he was hanging out in spirit with all of us there, in that church, sporting a very huge grin.

God bless all of those young men. What courage it must have taken for each of them to stand up in front of twenty-five hundred people and pour their hearts out, as they did, for all to hear. Mostly, teenage boys are reticent to share anything with anyone except their very closest of friends, but this day—Andy's day—would be different.

We witnessed a sweet and touching surrender of their fears and inhibitions so that all of us might get even just a speck of the depth of friendship that each of them shared with our Sunshine. The stories shared brought much-needed laughter as we were transported back in time to the many exciting, yet sometimes dangerous, antics of these teenage boys. Our spirits were lifted for a moment and then—just like that, we were drawn back into the reality of our new lives without this beautiful soul whom we all loved so dearly and would deeply miss. Their heartfelt expressions of loss, and their tears, were proof of their unabashed love for and admiration of Andy. Theirs was clearly an indelible, unbreakable bond that they knew would never be severed—not even in death. In fact, time would eventually tell that Andy's death made their bond all the stronger.

We ended the service with each of our family members sharing our own touching tributes and professions of deep love for Andy. We shared who he was to us as individuals, and as a family, and who he'd continue to be until that glorious day that we'll all be joined with him again, in Heaven.

It's been said many times that "it takes a village." For this lovely and one-of-a-kind service, so many invested their hearts, as well as their time, to make this beautiful celebration of life one that truly represented just who this Andy kid was. For me "The Dance," a song made famous by country singer Garth Brooks, best represents how I felt.

Even if I'd have known how quickly life with my son would come to an end, I would never have chosen to miss one second that I was blessed to have with my beloved Andy. The pain that I live with now is well worth any amount of time I got to spend laughing with, and enjoying, my precious boy. Honestly, Andy lived more life in his sixteen years than most people live in sixty. The joy, the love, and the unadulterated happiness that Andy brought into our lives far surpass the pain that remains now, in his absence.

6

THE POWER OF THE MIND

With the passage of time, certain moments have become so precious and memorable to me. I remember images and events from my life now as if I had taken snapshots of them with the clearest of lenses; more beautiful, vivid, and colorful than ever before. These days, I notice the color of the sky and the shape and movement of clouds in ways that I never had before.

Most days, the radio is playing in my truck—Andy's truck—the windows are rolled down, and I am living right here, right now, in this moment. And even though I still miss my son, I often realize that at this specific time, on this particular day, I am feeling peaceful, joyful, and appreciative of all my surroundings. I don't feel the urge to hurry my life along or do anything else other than just drive down this road, reveling in these moments of pure beauty and peace.

Oh, how I love that inner calmness when it shows up. One of the most important things I do now is to stop, validate that wonderful feeling, and etch it into my memory as another moment to cherish. Carpe Diem! (Seize the day!) Note that it is a verb—an action, not a reaction.

So many times, after we lose someone we love, we sit around waiting to feel this or that, when in actuality we have to go out and create that feeling which we are seeking. I often say, "Peace, Joy, and Happiness don't just show up and knock on our doors; we have to leave our homes to go out and seek them." We have to be their creator. Then we need to accept and appreciate those feelings for what they are, for however long they are around, because at any given moment, they may vanish and be replaced by the nagging pressures and challenges of our daily lives.

Even in the state of shock I was in, I can still remember, clear as a bell, events and conversations from that first night that Andy left us. Some things are actually too clear and painful, and I have to push them away and replace them with better memories. In the beginning, this can be such an exhausting process because these images and memories are bombarding us at lightning speed all day long. Every corner we turn holds reminders of something else about our loved ones that we miss.

Dealing with these painful mental pictures was something that I either had to learn to manage or risk living in a state of constant horror for the rest of my life. There are times that I will literally shake my head as if to shake the thoughts and images away and out of my mind. But I've trained myself over the years that as soon as a disturbing thought or memory pops into my head, I quickly replace it—or reroute it—with one of my happy times spent with my son.

I have recalled and then tucked away some very special times and experiences with Andy that bring me joy, and I use them to replace the more painful memories when they arise. One such event is the red-letter day that Andy had pitched for the baseball scouts who were representing colleges, universities, and pros, when they were all gathered behind the backstop with their radar guns. I will never forget the smile and sheer joy on Andy's face as he leapt off the pitching mound and joined his other teammates back on the sidelines.

Another time I like to revisit is when Andy and I spent the day on a boat with his girlfriend Katie and both of her parents. Andy had been out on the lake many times before with Katie and several of their friends and had become quite proficient at wake boarding. He'd purchased a beautiful board with birthday money he had saved, and also a really cool life vest, both of which were the envy of many of his friends. Always the elite athlete, Andy mastered landing a backflip on that very wakeboard fairly soon into that summer. While I wasn't always thrilled to watch some of my son's daring tricks (they scared me), I sure loved seeing him delight in all the fun and beam proudly with his sense of accomplishment.

One Sunday afternoon, Andy cheerfully persuaded me to get up on his wakeboard while he and Katie were videotaping this momentous event. While I'm never one to shy away from trying new things and I've always been a pretty good athlete, I was fifty-two years old, after all, so at first this seemed to me a bit challenging. But less than a minute later, into the water I went.

I will always remember Andy's face and his shrieks of encouragement as I did, indeed, majestically rise up out of the water on his wakeboard. He and his girlfriend were both so delighted for me and cheered me on excitedly as I maneuvered my way across the wake as the water behind the boat parted way.

Just about the time I started relaxing and felt a little more confident in my new sport, BOOM! Down I went. Katie's dad swung the boat around quickly and Andy and Katie snatched me up out of the water, onto the boat, to save me from my watery grave. I somehow managed a half-assed smile as my very proud son cheered me on for my death-defying accomplishment. Seeing how proud he was of me warmed my heart. I thought I'd never stop smiling that day. Andy added music to the video of my infamous romp on his wakeboard, and we watched it together every chance we could, and laughed. Watching that video later, after Andy moved, and reliving those fun-filled moments with him, has pulled me up out of the blues on many occasions. I will always remember that day with such fondness.

As an aside, I describe Andy's passing as his having "moved." This reflects how I choose to perceive his lack of physical being. Andy is not lost, nor is he dead. Rather, he has simply moved to another dimension and I will surely see him again one day. This knowledge not only gives me great peace, but it also allows me to feel hope.

Another memory I cherish involves the trip Andy and I took down to Tucson, Arizona, for the annual baseball scouting weekend for high school juniors—something Andy and his teammates had prepared for since they were freshmen. Even as a small child, he had always been thoughtful and was usually the first person to offer help to another. But what Andy did during this trip went far beyond what most of us would likely do for someone else, especially a perfect stranger.

Picture this scene with all of these talented young men from all over the country spending the entire weekend in front of numerous baseball scouts, hoping upon hope to be noticed, moms and dads in tow cheering them on. There was such excitement and anticipation as these boys took the mound, pitched their best stuff, and hit and fielded the ball like champions.

As lunchtime approached, all the parents began making plans to feed their kids, and some of us headed off to Subway to pick up sandwiches and drinks. After standing in long lines, due to the crowds of people, we finally headed back to the field with our food and waited for the lunch break to be called.

As Andy came off the field and ran over to the spectator stands, he announced to me that I needed to go back to buy more food because this one kid from out of state was all alone and had no one with him to get him food or hang out with him. I told Andy he was nuts if he thought I was going back to stand in that long line again, and I meant it.

Andy motioned for the kid to come sit with us and began dividing his food up between himself and this other boy. As he finished eating, Andy asked if I could help the boy move to our hotel so that he wouldn't have to be lonely. After speaking to this boy's parents on the phone, long distance, and getting their permission to do so, we moved him from his hotel to ours. Staying in the same place with all the other boys made him feel safer and like he belonged to this group of strangers.

To top off the whole weekend, as Andy was on the pitching mound throwing his best left-handed sliders while several of the scouts and coaches stood watching, I saw him talking to one of the coaches. Then he ran off the field, and a few moments later, brought one of his friends, who was also a pitcher, back with him. Andy proceeded to tell the coach that this kid was really good and that they ought to watch him throw the ball, too. I guess he figured there was plenty of room in the baseball world for both of them. Andy had such a big heart and never let his own ego get in the way of anything.

We drove home at the end of the weekend knowing that Andy's future had finally begun in earnest. He talked endlessly about wanting to go pro, and how willing he was to train and do whatever it took to manifest that dream. He was never afraid, nor did he ever grow tired of doing the hard work necessary to master his baseball skills. In fact, I saved a voicemail from Andy which he left me on April 30, 2012, just seven and a half months before he moved to Heaven, which drove home that very thing:

Hello, it's your Sonner, and I don't know but today I had a good day at baseball practice, and I don't know why but I just did! And um, I don't know but today was just a really good day. And then I was talking to Damien about it and for some reason today the intensity level of me wanting to go pro intensified like twenty-thousand times more than it ever has, like I don't know what happened but honestly it makes me want to do like every single fricking thing possible to go pro, like anything, like all I want to do is eat, sleep, and breathe baseball right now. Just thought I'd like to let you know, so all right, Adios, love you, bye!

What in the world made me save that wonderful voicemail? In fact, by the time Andy passed, I had stored on my phone seven precious messages from my son. None quite as chatty as that one, but nevertheless all remain timeless treasures that I hold very close to my heart. Did I know, somewhere deep inside of me, that my time with Andy was limited? Or was it just a fluke that I saved them?

I remember quite clearly how much the first message from Andy amazed me because he was sharing his passionate heart with me—his mom—with such depth. Something that is such a rare occurrence for a teenage boy. Mothers generally have to guess what's going on in their kids' heads, but I thought I never had to. Thank God I saved all those voice mails.

On days when I'm struggling with my emotions and painful snippets that bring me right to my knees, memories like those just mentioned are the mental video clips that I run as an antidote through my mind. Without fail, they always bring a smile to my face and alter my current course of emotions for the better. I have used this technique over and over throughout my season of grief, and with great success. In fact, it is now nearly impossible for me to reflect on any of the difficult times I've had with any longevity because my mind has been trained to transport me instantly back to my happy memories. The power of the human mind is amazing, and I have given mine a workout, for sure. Surviving the loss of Andy has brought with it, for me, a whole new understanding of the true nature and meaning of mental toughness.

7

I'M A RISER

I start this morning just like I do every other morning since Andy relocated to Heaven, mapping out the day and trying my best just to live. Living used to be so simple. In fact, I never thought about it much at all before. It's not that our lives didn't have their challenges, but we seemed to be able to cope with things as they arose. Probably, it was easier to deal with the ups and downs of life because the scale never seemed to be tipped in one direction for very long.

All the typical things that we anticipated in a marriage and when raising children came along; colicky babies, ear infections, disagreements over money, changes of jobs and homes, not making the sports team at school, not being asked out for prom, illnesses and surgeries, and so on, ad infinitum.

All these things we have seen our parents and even some of our friends go through, which gave us a guiding light to follow and emulate. We knew instinctively that we'd survive, and we believed that the old clichés of "time heals all wounds" and "nothing lasts forever" had to be true.

Obviously, those who had coined those phrases had never lived through the loss of a child. I often tell people, "I don't have the flu or a broken bone. No. I lost my child. This one will not heal or go away, ever!" The thought of losing a child is unthinkable for any parent, until it happens. Our brains and hearts won't allow us to even conceive of it.

For all of those well-meaning friends who tried convincing me that they understood how I was feeling, it just isn't possible for anyone to understand what it truly feels like to have your heart ripped out of you if you haven't been there yourself. I wouldn't wish this journey on anyone, anywhere in the world, let alone my friends. I don't believe there is any way to prepare yourself for a tragedy such as this, other than to lay a firm foundation of coping skills that you've developed along the way of tackling life's normal, everyday struggles.

Nowadays, even given the deep pain I have felt, I often find myself experiencing true feelings of joy, laughter, and happiness—even in the midst of all the grief. At first, after Andy's passing, I couldn't even think about smiling or laughing again over anything. It seemed, in a way, disloyal to Andy and to the memories I hold so dear of our years together.

That attitude continued on for several months. Then somewhere along the journey I realized I'd given myself permission to live life again, to be happy, and that I would not be dishonoring my child in Heaven by doing so. In fact, I'm sure that our kids in Heaven want nothing more for us than to love and laugh again. For quite some time, I shared my sadness and pain with anyone and everyone who would listen, even with perfect strangers. I wanted them all to know the depth of the love I have for my son. I wanted people to know that my world had ended, and I really didn't know if I could go on.

As the years have passed, I've been able to find ways to help me live each day one moment at a time. More often than not, I start out with a pretty good outlook on life. Not sure why or how this has happened, but I no longer question it. I seize it! Most days, no real pangs of pain grip me, and I find myself actually looking forward to doing fun things—like camping with Clay and heading to San Diego with my girlfriends.

I am a creature of habit. Typically, my daily routine consists of making beds, breakfast, and spending quiet time alone, which involves doing my Bible studies and meditations. Then I catch up on Facebook.

Recently, I came upon a post by a dear, sweet friend that not only took me aback, but it really got my goat. She is always notoriously chipper—which is fine, albeit a bit annoying—but for some reason this post really bothered me, and I felt compelled to comment.

She was talking about the importance of surrounding ourselves only with people who lift us up and always have positive attitudes about life. She went on to quote a very famous female celebrity who'd said that exact same thing, as if to validate the point of view my friend was espousing. In my post, I said that I love her, but that I totally disagreed with her perspective—which she is, of course, entitled to have. I went on to say how deeply thankful I am for the courageous friends who've stayed by my side for the past three-plus years, which I knew could not have been easy.

One snarky woman responded to her post by saying, and I quote, "Yes, surround yourself with people who lift you higher, don't forget about the others but distance yourself from them." Really? That's what we're supposed to do—distance ourselves from people who are hurting and in great pain? Well, I hope that neither of them ever finds themselves in a position of need because I feel certain that their fair-weather friends will be incapable of either helping or supporting them in their times of crisis.

Many of my friends found it hard to call or visit, often unsure of what kind of mood I might be in if they did. For so long, my moods were all over the place. One minute I'd be crying and the next all excited about a new movie or a book that had just come out. I'm sure that, at times, I was the most depressing person to be around.

It's shocking for me to admit this, but many times I would voice, to my trusted friends, a real desire to end my life. I would even describe in detail how I planned to accomplish my own demise. Honestly, I wouldn't be here today if it hadn't been for a few brave friends who never deserted me and had the depth of character to love and support me through everything, no matter what.

Then the question became, what do I do to get myself out of this terrible funk? I needed to shake off the frustration that I was feeling and put myself back into a better, more peaceful state of mind. Immediately, I headed out to the gym where, with exercise, I could release any negative energies and redirect my difficult emotions. This has definitely become one of my favorite and most effective methods of coping with my sadness and/or anger.

For the first couple of years, I couldn't even go to the gym because I didn't have the energy required to work out— physically or mentally. I felt drained all the time, just trying to survive. Slowly but surely, though, I began to regain energy, and along with it, a desire to strengthen my body and mind. Finally, I felt ready to burn off some added pounds and release my anxiety.

Music is another important tool for me, especially when I'm in the gym. Usually, as I step onto the treadmill to begin my warmup, I pop in my earbuds. I have loaded onto my phone a few playlists of songs I like, especially for use during my workouts, that I use to help empower and encourage me.

One recent morning, with earbuds in place, I cranked up my music and got started. Although I was listening, I felt distracted by a difficult conversation I'd had earlier that day that was replaying over and over in my head. Then, one of my favorite songs by Dierks Bentley, "Riser," came on, and I was reminded of who I am.

The lyrics affected me to the depths of my very soul. They reached down deep within me and ignited a great surviving spirit inside. Feelings of thankfulness, gratitude, and strength poured through me. I felt myself surrounded by a spiritual whirlwind that had transformed my once-sullen state of mind into something both calming and magical.

Not only did I feel Andy's presence at that very moment, which was where some of my gratitude came from, but I also sensed the enfoldment of an Angelic presence as it infused me with love and hope.

Moments like these don't happen all the time, but when they do, they are transformative. I was grateful—and ready for the rest of the day.

8

Siblings

Our family began with the union of Clay and me. After four years of dating, we married on May 31, 1980, and we've been happily together ever since. Clay is ten years older than me, which has proven to be exciting and, at times, also challenging.

Throughout the years, our age difference has been a blessing and a hindrance due to the natural stages of life that we each go through. Sometimes, his age offers wisdom beyond my years, and other times, it's more like a parent telling a child what she ought to do. All in all, though, we have weathered our differences whenever they arose. They've not only strengthened us but bound us together in ways that cannot be broken. We realize how very fortunate we are. Marriages of many couples who've sustained this level of loss have been shattered and have not survived the devastation.

In a tragedy such as ours, it's important for the sibling voice to be heard since most of the support and focus usually goes toward the parents. Even the siblings are inclined to caretake their parents long before ever acknowledging their own silent struggles with loss. As such, the siblings will often struggle with this throughout their lifetimes, and typically with no real outlet for processing their own pain.

Even in close-knit families such as ours, this can lead to a very dysfunctional family, which only compounds the grief. Divorce, separation, and even additional suicides are all potential outcomes for families in the aftermath of suicide. I've found often that family members are the worst at helping each other through a tragedy like this, due to the intense pain that each person is feeling around his or her own loss.

Within our own families, we are often incapable of taking care of each other on the massive scale that's required following the tragic and sudden death of a loved one. And this only amplifies the need for a strong source of good friends and support outside of our own close circles of relatives. Yes, we need each other, but it is difficult for us to care for each other's needs every time they occur. Within our immediate family, we now have a sibling who, sadly, will not talk to any of us, and another who had turned to substance abuse—neither of which is a healthy response to the pain.

Running from grief, whether physically or emotionally, only buries it temporarily; there will be no healing that way. Only time will tell how it turns out for my family, but I am hopeful and pray each day for a deep healing within all of us.

By the time our son Michael was five, I had learned to regularly consult a great book called, *The Strong-Willed Child*, by Dr. James Dobson, founder and president of Family Talk, a Christian non-profit ministry. For me, this eye-opening book summed up who this marvelous child was and still is. Michael was definitely in charge of our lives from the start; just ask his siblings. So much talent and potential all rolled up into one kid, but wow was he ever a handful!

Michael was always at the top of his class in school and easily excelled on all the sports teams, both of which made him a pretty popular kid. Until high school, that is. He was a late bloomer in terms of height. As such, he felt insecure and began to struggle. Kids can be so mean, and Michael certainly experienced his share of being bullied.

Despite those early difficulties in school, Michael continued to be a high achiever, which ultimately allowed him to graduate a year early with a full scholarship. He couldn't wait to escape high school, where life was just a little too tough for his comfort. But again, we can't run from our problems. If we try, they just follow us until we're ready to deal with them.

Michael's answer to pain was drugs and eventually alcohol, a wicked addiction he is still battling and recovering from now, six years after Andy's move as I write this. Sadly, the loss of Andy—the kid brother whom he adored—only gave Michael another reason to drink in an attempt to bury the pain.

Beth was a beautiful, curly-haired redhead with a heart of gold. She popped out of the womb a nurturer and lover of everyone. From the start, Beth and Michael were inseparable. They were also very compatible, since he wanted to be adored and she adored him. Beth was quite a chatty young child, so much so that when Clay would get home from work, I'd strongly suggest he take her for a nice long drive, so that my ears could attempt to recover.

For me, there was nothing better than having a little girl to fuss over. From the time she was three, Beth loved playing dress-up and fixing her hair, which became an obsession while she was in gymnastics. "Don't touch my hair!" was her mantra. Gymnastics soon became a serious passion that consumed her nearly night and day. That level of commitment was quite challenging for her to maintain, though, once she was diagnosed with Type 1 Diabetes at the age of eight. Managing food, working out, and occasionally spending time with her friends was extremely tough given the rigorous schedule that was required for being a competitive gymnast.

All the health-related challenges that Beth has faced have led her to being one of the most compassionate people I know, and really fostered her later career choice as a nurse—and maybe even a doctor someday down the road.

Beth's natural inclination to "mother" was apparent from her first years of life. Ultimately, she became a mom herself at the tender age of seventeen and produced three beautiful grandchildren for Clay and me. My daughter's nurturing spirit was never more apparent to me than when she painted the blue heart on the floor in Andy's room.

In addition to her loving nature, Beth was also a talented dancer who moved beautifully and with so much grace. She continued with dance and gymnastics until giving birth during her senior year. Amazingly, Beth managed to graduate from high school while taking care of her premature baby, who was born at just twenty-nine weeks. Nothing was going to stop our Beth from becoming the woman that we knew she was destined to be. These little siblings were the perfect start to our family.

Then came Josh, who would complete our brood—or so we thought. Josh's birth was every bit as easy as he was. I was sure that no gentler soul had ever been born. After all the ruckus of having our rambunctious toddlers, Clay and I really appreciated the calm, sweet disposition of our new addition. In keeping with his wonderful nature, Josh was also the comedian of the family, and later on he'd often be seen entertaining his schoolmates.

By age four, it became apparent that Josh was going to need glasses, and he was not thrilled. We learned to buy his glasses in pairs, as they always seemed to be disappearing. Looking out the kitchen window one day, watching the kids play, I saw Josh take off his glasses and proceed to bury them in the dirt with his toy tractor. *So, that's what happened to all of his other glasses!* No doubt, contacts were on the horizon for this clever kid.

Josh's love of music began at age eight, while he was playing in his elementary-school band. His talent and passion for music led to him being a leader in both the marching and jazz bands during high school. Josh was a friend to everybody and always made everyone smile with his charming personality.

The skills he'd refined in marching band would serve as a firm foundation for his personal development when he joined the Air Force. Josh would eventually become the Non-Commissioned Officer in Charge of Base Honor Guard, where he so proudly displayed his amazing talent for leadership and understanding of teamwork. While Josh has maintained his sense of humor over the years, his life has become more structured and disciplined due to the influence of his time spent in the military.

Unfortunately, structure and control seemed to be roadblocks for Josh in facing the loss of his little brother. I wish I knew what was going on in his head these days. If I did, maybe I could say or do something that would help. For some reason, Josh has shut all of us out of his life altogether.

The only thing that makes sense to me is this: that Josh eliminated all physical reminders of his cherished brother as the only way he knew how to deal with this enormous tragedy, at least at the moment. I pray each day without ceasing for this situation to change, but only time will tell. For me, it feels as if I have lost another son. The ache in my heart is excruciating and only compounds the existing trauma of having lost Andy.

Last but certainly not least, eleven years after Josh was born, our precious Andy made a surprise grand entrance into our hearts and lives. Clay and I found raising a child later in life to be far easier than it was the first time around. After already having lived through the antics of three other kids, nothing much ruffled our feathers. That being said, Andy didn't do much to upset the family flow. He melded into the group quite easily as we hauled him around to all the activities of his various siblings. That is, until his own life began taking shape.

Around the age of six, when Andy first started to play baseball, Clay became one of his very first coaches. This cemented even further their already tight father-and-son bond. This would become a great passion they shared right up until the day our Andy moved to Heaven. Andy loved baseball more than anything, and Clay loved Andy beyond measure.

Early on, Andy also took to Boy Scouts quite naturally. Never one to be content to just stay inside, Andy involved himself in every activity he could that would allow him to spend time outdoors.

By this time, Clay's schedule was much more flexible, so he became quite active with Andy's Boy Scout troops from the start. This allowed him to spend an enormous amount of time with his young son—and the two of them got along famously. They hiked, camped, kayaked, blew up rockets, and most importantly, developed a deep relationship that would one day help to carry Clay through the loss of his precious son.

9

HIS THINGS

Scrolling through the television channels, I paused to watch one of Andy's teammates, Cameron Ming, play in the College World Series for The University of Arizona. While I am extremely proud and happy for Cameron and his family, you can imagine the envy and pain that I felt. *Why isn't that my kid playing today?*

I used to dream of watching Andy on TV playing the game he so loved. One funny, sad, yet special fact is that Cameron now has the glove that Andy loved, had begged and pleaded for so unabashedly, and eventually got. Cameron is one of the kids that Andy spoke of so highly to the baseball scouts when they were both at that camp in Tucson, right before Andy left us for Heaven.

They're both left-handed pitchers, so I knew Andy would want Cameron to have his treasured glove and that Cameron would always cherish it. Cameron and Andy were best friends both on and off the baseball field and often spent nights at each other's houses. They enjoyed listening to classic rock together and eating tacos prepared by Cameron's mom, Susie. Andy loved her cooking, so more often than not their overnights were at Cameron's house.

One night after Andy had moved to Heaven, Susie sent me a picture of Cameron oiling that glove with all the love and care he could muster. It's such a bittersweet act of honor and expression of love. I hope that Cameron carries Andy's spirit with him wherever he goes. I think of Cameron often, and wonder if he continues to think about Andy. What goes through his mind whenever he puts that glove on his hand? Does it make him smile? Does it give him strength and courage? I don't hear from Cameron anymore, but I'm sure that the memory of his simpatico friend still pops into his mind from time to time.

As word got out about Andy's glove being given to Cameron, the phone began to ring with inquiries from some of his other close friends.

"Can I please come over and pick up something of Andy's that I can keep as a memento?"

This was the question over and over again. What an awkward thing for any parent to have to process. Of course, my answer was always "Yes," and without hesitation. But when the reality of these kids standing in Andy's room going through all of his things actually began soaking in, that was an extremely difficult pill for me to swallow. On one hand, I wanted them to take a "piece" of Andy that they could keep with them forever and hold dear. But on the other hand, those tokens were the only tangible "pieces" of my precious son I had left.

With trepidation, and yet with care, the kids opened Andy's dresser drawers and stood in his closet, while searching for just the right item as their remembrance. As they held his revered baseball jerseys in their hands, I could see by the expressions on their faces that they were remembering all the special times that they had shared with their best pal. It was heartbreaking to watch while a few of them breathed in Andy's scent as they raised his clothes to their faces. In that moment, all their pent-up tears began flowing. With each touching remembrance, the kids and I were learning to grieve and begin to process our pain. We did it that day together. The sacred time Andy's friends and I shared with each other in Andy's bedroom became the cement that would bond us to each other for life.

Andy's favorite baseball jersey went to Degan, his prized model replica of a blue Shelby Mustang convertible to Bryce, and memorabilia of their shared moments together went to Katie. His uncountable pairs of Converse shoes went to Andy's sister, brothers, and friends. Andy had owned just about every color known to man of the popular Converse Chucks. In fact, one black pair still sits on the floorboard of his pickup truck, exactly where he left them earlier on that fateful day. Andy had always carried an extra pair in his truck, to be worn after baseball practice ended. I've never wanted to move those shoes from exactly the place where he'd left them, so they remain. Strangely, I find an enormous amount of comfort seeing them every day as I climb into his truck and drive off.

Looking back, I can't honestly recall who all stopped by and what they took home with them. It was truly a painful process, and I tried my best to prepare myself in advance so that I wasn't a blubbering mess when the kids came over.

This "letting go" process taught me quite a bit about my ability to control my emotions whenever needed, and I also learned that I possess amazing resilience. I could see how much these things of my son's meant to each and every one of his friends, and to a certain extent (albeit small), I did find comfort in knowing that these special friends cared enough about Andy to want something personal of his to carry forward with them on their journeys through life.

Some of these friends, which included a few adults, still send me messages and/or pictures of the cherished items they received during those first tough couple of weeks. I'm so glad that I was able to release my hold on Andy's possessions so they could be shared. I remind myself often that *Andy is not his things, but rather a beautiful soul who still shares a spiritual space with me.*

The human mom, however, still likes to smell, feel, and touch the clothes that Andy wore on that last day. I've tucked them away in a bag so I can preserve his special scent that only I, his mother, can identify.

10

LIFE GOES ON

Whether we wanted it to or not, Christmas came fourteen days later. Our grandchildren waited guardedly for a sign from Clay and me that it was okay to celebrate and be joyous. Children appear able to process grief in a simpler way than adults, or so it seems. It's not that the grandkids weren't sad, but they were eager to get on with life as it was. I believe it's due to their limited life experiences that they didn't have the ability to fully express their thoughts and feelings relative to losing their uncle, whom they adored.

As time has gone on, I have seen the grandchildren reflect upon their Uncle Andrew, but it's always with joy and laughter about the fun or funny things that he did. I like to think it's because Clay and I have never stopped talking about Andy, even from the very moment he left us, that they're able now to share their own fond remembrances of him, too.

Clay and I set the tone in the family for picking up the pieces and going on. We treasured Andy's memory and would speak about him often, rather than dwelling on how he transitioned from Earth to Heaven. We never sugarcoated the way Andy died because we wanted everyone to learn from our tragic experience and for this to not be repeated. Suicide is how he died, not who he was. His means of death does not define the loving person that was our Andy. We quickly learned that we could respond to tough events with either fear or action, and that we got to choose whether to be victims or victors. I was determined to own this grueling journey rather than allow it to own me.

That first Christmas was difficult, but it paved the way for many more firsts to come. We stayed true to our annual rituals as best we could, so that our kids and grandkids would feel safe, valued, and loved. It's easy to get so lost in mourning the departed that we forget to celebrate those who are still living. They needed to know that they, too, were important to us, and that we treasured their presence in our lives.

On Christmas evening, as we were doing our best to keep our difficult emotions in check, an unexpected visitor named Michelle arrived at my door and—even up to this day—she has never left. Well, she did eventually return home, but she continued showing up at my house day after difficult day and we grew quite close. Michelle is the mother of Bryce, one of Andy's best friends. She and I hadn't really met before that day, as our boys were older when they became friends, and the need to investigate our kids' friends and their families had diminished as they grew up.

Michelle later told me she had been in the middle of fixing Christmas dinner for her family and a houseful of people when she felt a very strong urge to immediately pay me a visit in my home—a spiritual force was beckoning her to my door. Moments later, as she was driving nervously to my house, she engaged in "conversation" with Andy—whom she adored—pleading with him for guidance about what to say to me when she reached my home. Terrified as she was about what my response might be to her unexpected intrusion, she rang the doorbell.

I am so thankful that Michelle had the spiritual insight to hear and then the courage to act upon what had been a Divine nudge to come to my aid. Michelle was the first of a small group of repeat comforters that I would come to rely upon. Disappointingly, those who had been my "best friends" prior were too fearful or self-involved to set aside their own sadness—even if just for one hour—and reach out to comfort me. Those folks literally fled the scene, never to be heard from again.

I have certainly learned a lot about human nature, courage, and love through this arduous journey. My new friends, my very own first responders, were like firefighters rushing into the flames of my pain and sorrow without any thought or worry about themselves.

Gradually, as Michelle's trust of me and our new friendship grew, she confided in me something that had haunted her since she was a teenager. She, too, had experienced devastating trauma; her dad completed suicide when she was just sixteen years old. Her family had handled their loss in a different manner than ours, and it left her unable to fully heal.

Moving through our journey with us eventually provided Michelle with an outlet for beginning to process a deep wound that had not ever been addressed. Just the mere word suicide terrified her and was taboo vocabulary in their family. This new beginning for Michelle gave her a forum for processing her pain and tremendous loss, and she finally began to heal. Funny how the person who was comforting me and loving me so unconditionally was shown her own path down the road of recovery and into a whole new life. God sure works in mysterious ways.

I'm still as amazed today as I was back in the beginning by the kids who showed up at our house day after day. Sometimes they'd visit with me, but most of their time was spent hanging out in Andy's room—laughing, crying, and sharing their favorite stories about their best friend.

Even more surprising to me were the parents who weren't afraid to let their precious children hang out in a house where someone they knew had just died by suicide. Really, how would you feel about your kids? Wouldn't you be worried? Yet these parents seemed to understand there was something special occurring at our house that none of us could have ever foreseen. Somehow, in the midst of deep pain and sorrow, we were all learning how to hold each other up without any fear or shame. Even though they were mostly teenagers, nobody was ever too embarrassed to break down or cry.

We were fortunate to have learned something in the wake of this terrible tragedy that many people never learn in their entire lifetimes: empathy—real empathy—not fake platitudes, but real, genuine love and concern for another person. We have been gifted with the development of true compassion that would go on to serve us and others whom we would encounter along our lives' paths.

We weren't cognizant of this at all, but it was happening right under our noses. The more each of us talked and shared, the greater was our understanding of the many different ways people cope (or not) with loss and grief. There are no two methods of dealing with pain that are exactly alike.

Given the complexity of the human brain, it makes sense that there is no one right way of handling things. Obviously, some ways are healthier and more productive than others, but who is to say what will be helpful for one person versus the next? It's been my experience that only trial and error and lots of faith and persistent prayer helped me to start moving forward. I've had to use many different coping methods for dealing with Andy's death, depending upon the various situations I encountered and the mood or disposition that I was in.

Every day has been different. I'm very thankful that I had laid a foundation of coping skills years earlier, and that I knew myself very well as a result. It's difficult, if not impossible, to develop effective coping skills in the midst of a crisis. This arsenal for survival would come to save me on many occasions during the years following Andy's move to Heaven.

Hopefully, you have been preparing for whatever inevitable challenges you will face during your life's journeys. However, I pray that this particular challenge is one that you never have to face.

Rudy Bencomo
12/14/99 - 8/4/17

Owl Always
Love you....
Madre

11

SPIRITUAL VISIT

There were many blessings along the way, some almost immediately. While I am a woman of deep and profound faith, when one's life is shattered like mine, all resiliency is tested. Thankfully, for me, I had signs that Andy did, indeed, live on—"sign[s], sign[s], everywhere a sign," just as it says in the popular seventies song "Signs" by Five Man Electrical Band.

I always believed that Heaven existed, but when I lost my child, everything I thought I knew was suddenly called into question. Having been raised in the church, I believed as I was taught—that one day we'll all go to Heaven (or at least most of us), but that was just an elusive concept that had no relevance in my life—until now. I needed to know what that place called Heaven was really like, the place where my Andy was surely residing. Amazingly, almost immediately after he moved upward, Andy showed up for Clay and me in the most beautiful and unexpected way.

We were still in bed very early on the second morning after Andy's relocation, but we were both already awake. Clay suddenly said, "Do you see him?"

"Yes!" I whispered cautiously, so as not to scare him away. Andy's spirit was a rich blue hue and was standing at the foot of our bed hovering over us, as if to cover us and comfort us with all his love. Clay and I held each other and wept while our precious boy "laid" on top of us for several minutes. We knew instinctively that Andy was letting us know that he was all right, and that he would continue to be around and share in our lives. Yes, it would be different from what we had hoped for, and planned for, all of his life, but it would just have to be enough. Somehow, we both knew that it would be.

When I used to tell that story to people, they tried hard to convince me that it was just the wishful imagination of grief-stricken parents. But without a doubt, Andy's spirit was with us that morning in our bedroom, and we'll never forget it—and he would visit us again, as time went on.

The next several years were an awakening of sorts, for me. In retrospect, it appears to me that I had been sleepwalking through life prior to Andy's move to Heaven. Yes, I was spiritually awake on some levels, but I realize now that I had missed so many great opportunities to experience a life far richer than what I could have ever imagined.

Granted, I would go back in a heartbeat to who I was before, if it meant I could have my son back. But that was clearly not possible. My only choice was to move forward, which I reluctantly did. Then backward, then forward again. This was to become the new rhythm I danced with me, myself and I. Some days I'd move with relative ease, and other days I'd step all over my own toes and fall flat on the floor.

The subtle (and not quite so subtle) signs along the way, and the new people I met and befriended, were guideposts to help me navigate my way through this new maze of uncharted waters. Nature seemed to be screaming at me so I would not miss one single thing. Sunsets, clouds, butterflies, birds, trees, flowers, and more, all of these wonders came to life right in front of my eyes with vivid colors and vibrancy, all announcing themselves to me like trumpets announcing the arrival of Andy in Heaven.

When I looked at the clouds lacing the sky at sunset, it dawned on me that the contrast of light and dark was what made them so beautiful. Without one counterbalancing the other, it would be an uninteresting, monotone sky. But with wind kicking up colored dust and with darkness looming, the sky would appear as a beautiful entryway up into Heaven. It beckoned me to look longer, and when I did, I was drawn into a spiritual realm that showered me with warm feelings of peace and love.

In those breathtaking moments, I could relax for that sacred time and fall safely into the arms of my Divine Source of all love and healing. As tender waves of comfort washed over me, the heavier feelings of grief and loss I'd been carrying began to release. I had witnessed many beautiful sunsets in the past, but now the night skies sprang to life with a whole new meaning. God was speaking to me through this gorgeousness, and Andy was sitting right next to me, gazing at the wonders of our Creator.

As I soaked up these universal spiritual offerings, a new energy emerged and began flowing through me like a gentle brook. Did I experience this every day? No. But I deeply treasured those nourishing and nurturing moments whenever they came. They were the sustenance that my body and broken spirit had so desperately needed. These moments miraculously transformed me into a woman of great power, strength and courage—attributes I had never before known I possessed.

Almost daily, the birds would sing sweet messages to me from Heaven. Cardinals that I had never noticed before suddenly began appearing in the trees and bushes outside my home. Red-tailed hawks followed me around the neighborhood and floated above my truck as I drove down the road. Rainbows showed up just when I needed a little extra faith to believe in life beyond here. Angels sent me heartfelt messages through the clouds, with shapes and designs so breathtakingly beautiful that they could only have been sent from Heaven above.

It's not that I never noticed these kinds of things before Andy moved, but now they had such a profoundly deeper meaning and connection. Was I imagining it? Who knows— and who really cares? They were giving me life-sustaining energy and the hope I so desperately needed. There was wondrous beauty in the world, even in the midst of my greatest tragedy. I only had to open my eyes and ears and allow it to permeate the grief shield I had surrounded myself with before, in the early days.

But this was just the beginning of good things to come and the tip of the iceberg that would lead to my spiritual awakening.

12

THE MEDIUM

"You need to see Susanne Wilson, The Carefree Medium" was the random message I received several times in my email and Facebook Messenger almost immediately after Andy's move to Heaven. *Are you kidding me? Don't people know that I'm a Christian and that we're told over and over never to consult a medium—it's of the devil?!* In all honesty, I'm sure I said that to many people over the years, too. But consult a medium I did.

While my faith was deeply imbedded in my entire being, I was desperate to have a talk with my son and know firsthand that he's okay. While I had been content with Heaven being a place where some of my relatives had already moved to and that one day I also would, everything had completely changed for me, perhaps even my entire belief system. I was willing to take a chance, even if that meant being open to seeing beyond what I had been taught all those years in church.

I secretly googled Susanne Wilson to make sure that she was as reputable as possible, given my belief that all of that woo-woo stuff was corny and even dangerous. I made sure not to tell anyone for fear of a reprimand or shameful lecture. I could already hear them in my head: Where is your faith, LeAnn? You'll be talking to evil spirits, or worst of all, you are definitely going to Hell.

I didn't care. I needed to talk with Andy. After doing my research, I made an online appointment using a different name so that she couldn't google me, and voila, I had a date in January, only forty days after Andy passed—just like the flood in the Bible.

As the date approached, I became apprehensive and asked my daughter, Beth, if she would go with me, just in case a spell would be cast over me while there. I needed someone to drive me home if I became incoherent or despondent. To my surprise, Beth was excited and eager to come to stand guard over me. For fear of being excommunicated from my church and family, I made Beth promise not to tell anyone.

So far so good. Normal office building with a nice waiting room. Beautiful pictures on the walls and serene music playing in the background to soothe us. Mini fridge stocked with water and a hot tea machine for nervous stomachs, or so I surmised. Even though I was scared, I felt a twinge of hope at the possibility of connecting with Andy again in a genuine way.

Within minutes, the woman that I had googled entered the room, and she changed my life forever. Susanne introduced herself and shook my hand, and much to my amazement, I didn't turn into anything scary. After a quick hello, she told my daughter that she could wait for me in the lobby, but that I had to go with her into her office alone. I had come this far and wasn't going to leave now, so into the back room I walked, with my digital recorder in hand. I was more than half serious when I thought, *at least this way there will be a record of my last words before I tragically disappear from this Earth.*

Susanne asked me not to tell her anything but to acknowledge when her information from Spirit was correct. She seemed like a lovely person from all appearances, so I turned on my recorder and waited for Andy. She led with a prayer and a grounding exercise before we began our conversation with the Other Side.

Almost immediately, Susanne said, "I have a young man here who has very recently passed." She continued with precise details of how he had moved to Heaven, and quickly told me that my son was so glad that I was here to visit with him. Tears began to fall down my cheeks as I waited for more information.

Andy told me, through Susanne, that his blood had been poisoned and that he wasn't thinking clearly on the day that he shot himself. He told me that it wasn't my fault and that I couldn't have known what was happening any more than he could. When Andy said that his blood had been poisoned, it all began to make sense. Andy had been taking the prescription drug Accutane before he passed, for treatment of acne. It had affected his ability to think clearly and caused him a great deal of confusion.

Susanne could not have known that shortly before our session, Andy's dermatologist had called to express his deepest condolences and inform me that he had reported to the FDA that Andy's suicide had been caused by the Accutane. Wow, talk about a shocker.

And talk about feeling like a horrible parent. I had signed the waiver in his office for this drug that said, "Suicide, psychosis or depression are potential side effects." I had never given it a second thought, as I just assumed that those side effects pertained to someone who was already predisposed to depression—which was *not* my happy, well-adjusted kid. Besides, I'm a good mom and would have surely known if there was something horrible happening to my child.

My mind immediately began to recall the subtle signs of this lethal drug's interaction with my son. *Oh my God, how could I have been so blind?* Hindsight might be 20/20, but I would have to live with this now for the rest of my life.

Susanne and Andy nudged me back to the present tense, reiterating that it wasn't my fault that he had ended his life. Through Susanne, my son eagerly told me there were big things ahead for me to accomplish—and that I would do them with Andy's help. His final words through Susanne were, "My mom is tough as nails, and she'll be fine!"

My conversation with Andy lasted one glorious hour. It filled my heart and renewed my spirit. As the session was winding down, Susanne told me that Andy had gone out to the waiting room where my daughter was and that she was talking with him. *What? My daughter sees and hears from the dead? No, not possible. I swear, she was perfectly normal when we arrived.*

That day was the beginning of an awakening that would open my heart and soul, so that I could minister to thousands of other bereaved parents and kids through a foundation that I didn't even know I was about to create. Andy would continue to guide and encourage me with his humor and love in the weeks, months and years to come.

13

HELPING PARENTS HEAL

Feeling just a tiny bit of relief after my first of several visits with Susanne Wilson (a.k.a. The Carefree Medium), it was evident I needed to build on any progress I'd made thus far toward healing. I didn't even like to say the word "healing," as I never thought it would be possible to heal after the devastating loss of Andy.

It would be three years after Andy's move before I would cautiously allow myself to voice to others that indeed healing had begun.

Without a doubt, the most influential and pivotal person who provided a platform for this elusive journey toward my healthier, happier well-being was Elizabeth Boisson. She and Mark Ireland are the co-founders of the non-profit organization, Helping Parents Heal (HPH). HPH is a unique type of group, dedicated to assisting bereaved parents by providing support and resources to aid in the healing process. Tragic as this is, HPH has 12,200 members worldwide and counting. And all are parents who have suffered the loss of a child, including both Elizabeth and Mark.

Thankfully, during the final minutes of my first treasured "conversation" with Susanne and Andy, Susanne had wisely suggested that I connect with her friend Elizabeth. I clearly remember Susanne encouraging me to reach out to Elizabeth and to Helping Parents Heal through the HPH website, as well as Facebook. Susanne said that it would change the trajectory of this ugly path I was on and would begin to allow my heart to be pieced back together.

The final words Susanne left me with were, "Andy wants this for you." At this point, I wasn't too sure that Andy should get a say in how I grieved. He couldn't possibly understand the absolute horror of losing a child. In addition, he was in Heaven where pain and sorrow are no more, while I was stuck here on Earth, feeling every gut-ripping emotion known to humankind.

Is healing even possible? And if so, what would that actually look like? Never having experienced any kind of loss in the past—much less one this enormous—it was clear to me that I was not at all equipped to answer these two questions. Without some assistance from others, I was ill-prepared to traverse this path of pain on which I found myself. I knew instinctively that I'd have to seek out other people who had survived this same kind of loss and hopefully garner some of their coping tools for my own use.

After finding the Phoenix chapter of Helping Parents Heal online, I noticed that the next monthly meeting was just two short weeks away. Can I possibly drag myself there and sit with so many other parents who I'm sure will look and feel as hopeless and lost as I do?

As the date got closer, from somewhere deep in my gut I felt compelled—almost commanded—to go. Maybe it was a nudge from Heaven to do something that clearly felt quite uncomfortable. I have never been much of a joiner or a group person. I have always felt most at home marching to the beat of my own drum. However, my drum had gone silent after Andy's passing, and I had no idea when or how a new sound would ever begin.

As I walked through the doors of The Logos Center, where the local Helping Parents Heal meetings were held, I glanced around the meeting room for other zombie parents. I noticed a lot of people talking and laughing. Have I arrived at the wrong place? There was certainly nothing to laugh about in my state of mind. Then, almost immediately, a beautiful, tall, almost glowing woman saw me enter the room and placed herself squarely in front of me. As she leaned over to embrace me and welcomed me to the group, I felt somewhat relieved to know that I might just be in the right place after all.

As this gentle woman introduced herself and her child to me, she lovingly asked me my name and the name of my child. Interestingly, I heard her ask who my child is and not was. She was speaking in the present tense as if he was still right here. Maybe she doesn't understand that Andy died?

After telling me about her precious son Morgan, and how he had... transitioned at Base Camp on Mount Everest, it was clear she understood that Morgan and Andy weren't here, at least in the physical sense. She was an odd one, to say the least, but oh-so-welcoming and friendly. To me, Elizabeth seemed like a beaming embodiment of a person—almost disconcerting in my state of being because she seemed way too happy to me.

Not wanting to chitchat with anyone else, I put on a name tag and took my seat among the other parents. It was surreal to find myself in a setting like this. It had only been seven weeks since Andy had moved to Heaven, so I was still in a state of shock and disbelief. I looked round the room cautiously, so as not to draw attention to myself. I could hardly believe that I was now part of this horrible club that no one in their right mind would ever choose to join.

Elizabeth stood up in front of the crowded room and welcomed everyone. She seemed so happy that we were all there, which I found to be quite strange. She spoke with a gentleness that somehow also exuded strength and comfort. Hers was the kind of voice that immediately eliminated any and all of my fears and defenses.

While I was extremely uncomfortable being part of a group setting like this, at least I knew that I was in the company of people who understood exactly what I was feeling. They had first-hand knowledge of this terrible path of grief and loss I was on. Our children had all passed because of different circumstances, yet we shared the universal experience of wholeheartedly missing our children.

After Elizabeth's introductory remarks it was time for us all to move into smaller circles and share with each other about our children. Apparently, I had missed reading the suggestion included on the HPH website that each of us brings a picture of our beloved child to the meeting. Lucky for me, though, I did have a number of awesome pictures of Andy stored in my phone, so I was still able to share my precious son with the group.

In many Native American traditions, a "talking stick" is passed from person to person during group gatherings, and only the person holding the stick, at any given time, is allowed to speak—and we had one such stick in each circle. As it was passed around mine, each parent shared about her or his child and how he or she passed over to the other side. Some sobbed through the entire process, while others somehow managed to get through these moments without shedding a single tear.

Listening to their various stories, I could see a correlation, for the most part, between the amount of pain displayed outwardly and the distance of time from the child's transition. This wasn't always the case, though, as some were still stuck in their grief even after several years. This was frightening for me to see and would become a great motivator for me. I had to figure out whatever I needed to do, so that a couple years down the road, I would not be in the same condition as I was that afternoon. I knew that I wouldn't—and couldn't—keep feeling this awful forever.

As hard, in some ways, as the meeting was for me to sit through, I knew that I needed to return the next month, even though I almost dreaded it. As uneasy as I felt participating in these monthly meetings, I knew in my heart of hearts I had found a place that offered hope toward a better tomorrow for all who attended.

As I continued attending meetings, I developed friendships with some of the other parents. My new friends and I were free to talk about our children without hesitation, and talk we did, sometimes for hours on end. Mostly, we didn't want our kids to ever be forgotten, and talking about them with each other helped to keep their spirits alive within us and all around.

The format and content of our meetings provided some obstacles for me to overcome. The talk of our children being right here, and the use of mediums and meditation, were all things that were downright forbidden by my Christian upbringing. But, just like my first meeting with Susanne Wilson, these were extreme circumstances that I believed required extreme measures.

I was willing, albeit reluctantly and with guilt, to continue traversing this unfamiliar territory if it meant I could find some relief from my constant pain. Eventually, I would reconcile my Christian faith with my new spiritual beliefs and find a blend of the two that I was comfortable settling into. This would be a long journey, though, and it required a

lot of prayer, meditation, and reading, because in the beginning, most of what was spoken about at the meetings was
completely foreign to me.

Ultimately, many of my Christian friends dropped out of
my life because of their narrow-minded belief that the way
I was beginning to think and talk about spiritual matters
was forbidden in the eyes of God and the church. But this
"loss" turned out to be a gift that arrived in a crappy-looking
package, because their exit allowed room in my life for new
friends who were supportive and loyal. They filled my heart
and life with much love as we navigated these choppy waters together.

As unsettled as I was at first with Elizabeth's whole demeanor, I couldn't help but feel comforted by the stirring of
hope brought on by her presence, as well as the love she exuded from every pore.

Later down the road, as I released my sorrow and traded
up for more love and joy, Elizabeth and I formed an indelible
bond. We also became the very best of friends, a blessing I
never saw coming.

Moving forward and eventually healing became a reality
for my life with the help of so many of the other great moms
and dads who are also a part of Helping Parents Heal. Little
did I know then all that was possible for my future and how
influential these relationships would come to be. These unbreakable ties became a life-sustaining force for me from the
start. Although I didn't realize it at the time, they were soon
to become my social circle.

14

SIGNS OF LIFE

After Andy moved to Heaven, I woke up each day feeling like I was living the movie Groundhog Day, in which a weatherman finds himself caught in a time loop, reliving the same day over and over again. I would open my eyes, look around, and realize this nightmare had really happened to me and my family. *How do I breathe? How do I live? How do I go on without my precious son?* Every day, I faced the same haunting questions and the same awful reality. Nothing would ever change, and I wondered, *is it even possible for my day to have any other kind of beginning or ending than this?*

While my visit with Susanne, the medium, helped, I was still faced with the reality of my heart being shattered into more than a million pieces. I was severely wounded by my loss, and I felt every bit of pain and sorrow that one person could possibly feel. I looked like a walking zombie—barely able to go through the motions, shuffling my feet back and forth in an attempt to get through the daily efforts required for my survival.

Then one day, much to my surprise and amazement, as I was standing in front of the bathroom mirror brushing my teeth, I noticed my body moving slightly to the beat of the music that was playing on the radio. *How dare I? Am I really going to allow myself to dance after losing my son?* I felt betrayed by my own heart.

As I continued observing myself, something occurred to me. *I must really want to live, or why else would I be dancing?* Was it merely just a physical reaction over which I had no control? Or was it something bigger... deeper? Was this my soul crying out to survive regardless of what my heart had to say about any of it? Like the fluttering wings of a baby bird as he learns to fly, I could feel the sensation of something new stirring within me.

I should stop this display of life before anyone walks in and sees me. Then another, more positive, thought came to mind. *But as long as I'm standing here at the mirror, should I fix my hair a little bit and put on some makeup?* I wondered what people might think if they saw me. *Remember, LeAnn,* I told myself, *you aren't the first mom ever to lose a kid and you haven't seen any other zombies lately, so life must go on after all. Anyway, maybe no one will notice if your appearance looks a little more present-able today than usual.* And really, who cares what anyone thinks, anyway? I was the one just hanging on by a thread while doing my very best to survive.

The next day arrived just as it had the day before. But this time, I opened my eyes, brushed my teeth, fixed my hair, and once again danced to the music. *What will be next?* I wondered. *Will I continue this crazy betrayal by my own heart? What about the gaping hole that's still there?* Was the song of my soul louder and stronger than the cry of my heart? Perhaps. Had the spell of *Groundhog Day* been broken? I sure hoped so.

As I continued to dance toward life, affirming every miniscule movement forward, all these questions and more began to race through my mind.

The early days, for me, were like ocean waves. At first, they crashed over my body relentlessly, pulling me all the way down to the floor of the sea, and thrashing me around. As time went on, there were lulls between the crashing waves that allowed me to rest for a while and catch my breath. It was during those brief periods of calm that I first spied a glimpse of the sun shining on the seas and sensed a renewal of my strength as I waited for the next rash of waves to come in.

Solid rest and hope became my life preservers, and I clung to both of them for dear life. I began to gain more confidence in my ability to survive the next barrage of grief and sorrow with the knowledge that the sun would indeed shine again and the waters would begin to calm down.

Eventually, I came to the place emotionally where I am now. The waves are much farther apart, and they only knock me under every once in a while.

Training myself to allow these valiant efforts of my soul to gain ground proved essential for my survival. I knew I needed to grab ahold of the lifeline that was being thrown to me from across the veil (of the afterlife). Yet this turned out to be something I'd have to fight for over and over again.

Throughout the years, I have heard many people spouting off about how miserable they are in their lives. While I am not belittling the depth of human suffering or the amount of difficulty inherent in daily living, I'm a big believer that life is exactly what we make of it. When I focused primarily on my pain and suffering, pain and suffering were all I could see and experience. Did I want more? Or did I need to be held hostage in my grief in order for people to recognize and understand my loss?

My actions spoke louder than my fear. I did want more. I wanted to live. Somehow our children are mistakenly connected in our minds to our grief process. As we move through that process, we're afraid of releasing the grief entirely for fear we'll also be releasing our children. For example, the first time someone asked me how I was doing and the word "Fine" spilled out of my mouth, it made my gut turn. The truth of my reply scared me, because I somehow believed that letting go of my pain and grief—even to some small degree—was letting go of all that I had left of my Andy.

Can death and life ever live side by side? A new soul song would have to be written for us that would echo our past, present, and future. If orchestrated with love rather than fear, it would be melodious and beautiful. Down deep, somewhere only my soul could hear, I knew that this was possible. It would take practice, patience, and perseverance, but when I listened closely, I could hear the music playing and the drums beating, calling me onward—albeit toward an unknown, unfamiliar place.

15

TIME TO GROW

I've tried my best to allow myself to take this spiritual journey at my own pace and to be open to Divine guidance along the way. I really had no idea what lay ahead. Do any of us? Ever? We try to plan and predict what possibilities lie waiting around the corner, but in the end, we are often surprised by the path our lives take and our ultimate outcomes.

As part of my own healing, I began to channel my energy into giving talks to parents who had also lost their children. In those presentations, I say that we can't always choose what happens to us, but we can and should choose how we respond. Being the control freak that I am, it was natural for me to want to be in charge of this whole journey of grief and healing, just like any other part of my life. I quickly learned that it doesn't quite work like that.

While everybody responds to tragedy and grief differently, most of us resort to our core personality traits to help us navigate through the rough waters of loss. Being in charge had always been my natural core personality, so it was reasonable that I would respond in this manner when Andy left. Even though that was my default response, I still had choices within that regarding what tools I would use.

For example, if you are more of a private person, you will be less likely to become a speaker or advocate like I have; rather, you may choose to move forward using a quieter process—perhaps by journal writing or blogging—which are still quite effective and healing. There are no right or wrong ways to cope, but some are healthier for us than others. Any behavior that does not allow or encourage us to process our grief and move forward can be considered unhealthy and is best avoided whenever possible.

The past two years have been jam-packed with adventure and change that have made it difficult for me to write. According to an old adage, we can't see the forest for the trees. I understand that now in a way that I hadn't quite grasped before. For a time, I was so focused on the trees that were deep within the forest of my survival that I didn't have any energy left for much else.

Four years after Andy passed, we sold our family home that Clay and I had built fifteen years earlier. The very one in which Andy had grown up, and where we had blossomed from six family members into twelve—adding three grandkids, two daughters-in-law and one son-in-law. It was also the home in which Andy died.

Not every parent responds to the death of his or her child the way I did. Some want to move away from their homes as fast as they possibly can, hoping they can put distance between themselves and their painful memories. For me, I found comfort being in the space where Andy grew up. This is where I felt most at home. It was our home, a place of solace and love.

I found it comforting to walk into Andy's room and reminisce about all the fun times he'd had there with all of his friends. I would lie on his bed, breathe in his scent that still lingered on some of his clothes, and give thanks to God for all the years I had been gifted with as his mom.

One day, as I was getting the house ready to sell, I realized I should probably paint Andy's room a more neutral color in order to make it more appealing to potential buyers. At the time, the walls were painted a very bright, deep blue, which just happened to be my son's favorite color.

As I gathered my courage to dismantle the physical memories still covering his walls, I happened to notice a series of tiny pin holes all over the ceiling. I grabbed the ladder and climbed to the top to examine these punctures a bit closer, and was suddenly struck with a vision that almost made me fall off the ladder, laughing. We had given Andy a dart gun one year for his birthday, and he dearly loved it. He would shoot his tiny little darts all over the house, which apparently had included his bedroom. I could just picture Andy with all his friends lying on the floor, having the time of their lives, and firing away at the ceiling while I slept peacefully in the room next to his—totally clueless.

As I was imagining this fun scenario, I said out loud to Andy, "I bet you guys had quite a blast in here. I can't believe you didn't accidentally shoot one another, or maybe you did and just laughed it off!" It gave me great pleasure to be connecting with Andy over this. I knew then, deep in my heart, that my boy had lived every second of his life. This was a powerful and profound healing moment for me. As I filled in the holes in the ceiling, it was like I was patching up some of the holes in my heart.

As we were in the process of selling our home and purging some of the more painful memories, a lot of other things happened. Clay was diagnosed with Stage 4 melanoma just six months after we lost Andy. Not long afterward, my mom moved to Heaven to be with her beloved grandson, we lost two of our daughters-in-law to divorce, nearly lost our oldest son, Michael, to alcoholism and PTSD, and lost all contact with our Air Force son, Josh.

It's nothing short of miraculous that Clay and I survived all of this in just a few years' time. Statistics aren't kind to any marriage after the loss of a child. Imagine what they must look like when coupled with all of these other tragedies. But survive we have. We have not only survived; we've thrived. No wonder I couldn't write for two years. I was being stretched and challenged to be a stronger, more resilient and loving LeAnn.

Never in a million years would I have ever believed that I'd become the person I am now. This has certainly been a progression, not always forward, but ultimately moving me toward a place where there is healing for me and others. I didn't believe that when this painful journey began, but it's important for me to look back and see the progression of my healing story—where I have come from and where I am today.

Some people never recover from tragedy. Instead, they just wander around like they're in the zombie apocalypse. Their bodies are here, but their souls have already left the building.

My prayer is that you will see hope in this process and can find comfort and encouragement for the path toward your own healing. I fought, fought, fought for my healing! I was determined to be alive emotionally and spiritually, much more than just simply physically. As Dylan Thomas so famously wrote, I did not "go gentle into that good night."

16

I WANTED TO DIE

As the weeks and months marched on after Andy's move, so did I. I made many decisions early on that would pave the way for me to ultimately become victorious over my sadness and fears. This does not mean that I don't still feel pangs of deep sorrow from time to time, but I am confident now they will pass. and my desire for life will continue to win over my fear of it.

After a time, fearing death was no longer a part of my thoughts, but fearing life was ever-present in my daily existence. Talk to almost every parent who has lost a child, and that is one of the first things that they all say—they no longer fear death. That's because death, in their minds, has just swallowed up their most precious and prized possession—their children.

If they aren't able to manage their grief and pain, this can be a very dangerous situation for many people. Scary as this may sound, death can appear to be a pleasant reprieve from the constant pounding of grief. And why wouldn't you want to be where your child is rather than this place, this often-challenging place that we call Earth?

While one might not choose to actively end one's own life, it can be just as deadly to passively not engage in living it. Essentially, you are breathing and functioning, but there is no joie de vivre—no joy of life left in you. I know, because I spent many of my early days after Andy's move existing in this very state of being. In fact, there were several times that I seriously contemplated ending my own life.

Many believe suicide is selfish. They wonder how you could possibly think about leaving behind the ones you love and causing so much pain.

On the logical side of the question, that makes so much sense—especially since we have already experienced first-hand the devastation of this kind of loss. Having thoughts of suicide, myself, I know that in those moments, you aren't thinking about anyone else, or anything else, other than yourself and your own excruciating pain. It's so unbearable and relentless that you just want to make the pain end. It's as exhausting as it is agonizing.

For me, walking up to the brink of death was shocking, as well as disturbing. How can I even think these things? Where in the world are these thoughts coming from? The bigger question became what am I going to do about this pattern of negative thinking? Decisions, decisions, yes, decisions; that is the key. I have a choice about what to do with my thoughts. Understanding the power of this saved my life. Clearly there is a difference between emotions and actions, and that's where my decisions come into play. On one hand, I felt like ending my life; but on the other, I could decide not to. This wasn't a passive journey. I had to be prepared in advance and have a plan for saving my own life.

During the early years, I would look death straight in the eye many times—never actually attempting, but coming too darn close. Each time I chose to live I felt more alive and more in control. Being the control freak I am, that was definitely helpful. I like being in charge of things, so why not be in charge of my life and the decision to go on living? Slowly but surely, as the days meandered forward, my desire to live strengthened and my knocks on death's door began to lessen.

Having a toolbox full of coping skills came in handy for the long journey that lay ahead. I learned, though, that I had to use them in order for them to be effective. It doesn't matter how many resources you have if they are not being utilized. You have to want to move forward. You have to want to want to live. And having a few good friends around to help you employ your resources is a plus, too.

There were times when I struggled to use my tools, but with friends around who offered them to me as needed, it became a little bit easier. Not only were they my helpful assistants, but they were also my trusted confidants.

I had a couple of friends, in particular, on whom I relied to be trustworthy with all the raw and real feelings and thoughts that ran almost constantly through my head. This was and still is, at times, a heavy burden for them to bear, but they don't seem to mind much at all. Seeking a counselor might be a better choice for most people, but my friends have lovingly encouraged me to unload all of my darkest thoughts onto their laps.

As time has gone on, the magnitude and frequency of my emotional vomit has decreased significantly, and I credit that to these selfless friends for their loyalty and bravery to the cause of sustaining me.

Thankfully, I had been acquiring many great coping skills—tools, as I like to call them—long before December 2012. Depending on the moment and what was needed, there were any number of tools in my emotional support toolbox that I would use. One tool alone would never have been enough to propel me forward to where I am now. Much like a car or truck, we can't possibly fix everything with one tool, so a good mechanic always has a variety on hand to use.

In any moment of crisis, it is extremely difficult, if not impossible, to find or develop lifesaving resources if you don't already have a few to fall back on. When I first began falling back, I found my pool of resources lacking, and quickly realized that I would need to obtain many more tools if I was ever again going to have a vibrant and fulfilling life.

I relied on a number of things to help keep my body, mind, and emotions healthy: spending time with friends, being outside in nature, engaging in meditation, prayer, exercise, yoga, listening to music, reading books, journal writing, and other activities. That first year alone, I read eighty books. Yes, really, eighty books. And none were on grief or sadness or suicide. They were all self-empowerment books— stories of other people who had triumphed over their personal tragedies.

I wanted to know how people overcame great sorrows and went on to live fantastic lives. Why in the world would I want to read about depression or grief? I was living it and I wanted out of it. I didn't need to know about the "five stages of grief." I went through all five of those stages every day, sometimes twice a day. Reading about how badly I already felt seemed, to me, like a morbid thing to do, and I wanted no part of it. But maybe that's just me.

Apparently, those types of books help some folks, as everybody and their brother wanted to give me one. As years have passed, I've continued to read, sometimes re-reading books I'd read during those first years, but not at the eighty-a-year rate that I had.

Many people who have experienced a trauma or tragedy have told me that no matter how hard they try, they can't read. Because the trauma has impacted the normal function of their brains, it's impossible for them to focus or remember anything for much more than a millisecond.

I definitely understand that difficulty since, even as an avid reader, I'd have to re-read paragraphs and chapters several times in order to remember what I had just read. But I always pushed through to the book's end. I've learned that if you want to move forward, you have to keep trying until you do.

As Winston Churchill famously said: "...never give in, never, never, never, never—in nothing, great or small, large or petty—never give in except to convictions of honour and good sense.'"

Holleh Javidan
September 11, 1985
April 17, 2012

My beautiful wonderchild

17

PLAY BALL

Baseball season began again in January 2013, just six weeks after Andy had moved to Heaven. Life was going to go on with or without me, particularly for the boys on Andy's high school baseball team. The players had collectively made the decision to dedicate the upcoming season to Andy, which I thought was quite brave and honorable. So, what would I do? What could I do? Could I possibly drag myself out to the games in an effort to support their endeavor? How would I sit in those bleachers and cheer them on? How would I even drive into the parking lot, let alone walk toward the field, without falling completely apart and crying my eyes out?

For me, the better and only real question became *how could I not?* If these young men had the courage to talk so openly about their friend, then I would somehow find the courage to show up and support them.

Within an hour after Andy passed, this team of players/ friends showed up at our front door distraught beyond belief, and I quickly found myself in the odd and uncomfortable position of being an example of bravery for them. Even then, I realized I was being given a gift—an opportunity to show this group of young men how to survive something you never want to have to survive, something that rocks your world.

As Andy's biggest cheerleader, and theirs, too, they were watching my every move and following my lead. Would the team and I hide our sorrow and put on a stiff upper lip? Would we fall apart and never recover? Or would we find a healthy way to grieve together and pull each other through toward a positive outcome?

The schedule was posted, and my calendar was set. "Play Ball" had always been one of my favorite mottos, and I intended to keep it that way. I loved the smell of the baseball glove, the seventh inning stretch, and the smoke from the barbecues grilling hamburgers and hotdogs. I had always loved every blessed thing about baseball, and the fact that Andy loved it as much as I did was icing on my cake.

As the first game approached, so did my fear. In some ways, going to watch the other team members play without Andy almost felt like a betrayal. But I knew Andy would want me there, and I had no doubt he would be there with us all in Spirit—probably sitting right next to me, up in the bleachers.

There are no words to adequately describe the kind of courage and determination it took for me to make my way out of my truck, *Andy's* truck, walk down the sidewalk, and climb up into the bleachers. As I made my way through the crowd of excited parents and fans, I could feel the eyes of everyone fixed squarely on me. *Breathe, LeAnn! Don't cry! Breathe!*

As I made my way to my seat, I couldn't handle all the well-meaning people who wanted to offer condolences and tell me "I'm sorry." All I could manage was myself. I was there to support these boys as Mama Hull, mother to their dear friend Andy, and that role was very sacred to me. Hard as it was, I wanted to be there for their season opener and lend support.

The moment the game began, the emotional cloud I had been under lifted—just enough so that I could get lost in the joy of my favorite game. My Sunshine Andy was surely there with me that afternoon, shining his divine light and love upon me.

I found myself cheering, screaming, and hollering like all the other proud parents, and I wondered if the onlookers thought my enthusiasm was as odd as I did.

I worried that my mere presence would cast a shadow over whatever event I'd happen to attend. Maybe the other parents were wishing I wouldn't show up, so that they could get on with their lives. I really had no idea. I pushed those thoughts aside because I was there for their boys and for myself—and also for Andy.

That process of making decisions to move forward regardless of how I felt proved to be critical in my learning about how much power and control I actually had over this journey. For the first few games, friends or family, or both, had escorted me. But as time went on, I found myself alone in this curious exploration of my human and mortal capabilities.

I wish I could say—and I am sure you would like to believe—that with time everything became easier. But the truth is it did not get easier with each passing game. The reality of my journey is that I made many decisions not based on how I felt, but rather on how I eventually wanted to feel. Those thoughts guided my actions, not my emotions. If it had been left up to my emotions, I would still be lying on the concrete where I had collapsed upon hearing of Andy's passing that fateful December day.

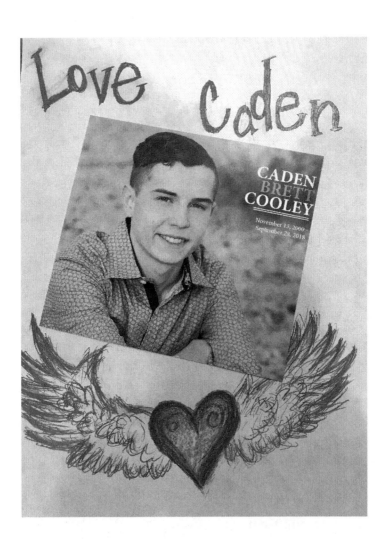

18

THE DRUG

One of the biggest and best decisions I made about what this path toward a new life would look like was whether or not to pursue legal action against the perpetrators of Andy's death. There were three different possibilities where legal recourse was a consideration. In the first couple of months after Andy passed, I met with seven different attorneys to determine if litigation was the correct remedy for our family to pursue. Thankfully, that would allow me some time to inch forward in the process and eventually make a healthy, life-affirming choice with the help of a seventh and final lawyer.

No one should ever have to go through this horrible process of interviewing attorneys after the sudden death of his or her child. The majority of the lawyers were not only compassionless, but blunt and oftentimes downright rude. How is a mother supposed to have that kind of a conversation with anybody after the tragedy of losing her child? What happened to empathy in our world? Where did that go?

I didn't want a check to "console" me because my son died, but I did want justice in his honor if foul play and negligence had occurred. Was justice even possible? What would justice look like? Was it necessary? Would it serve any purpose? Would I even know justice if I saw it? When I was finally able to answer those difficult questions, the path ahead of me became crystal clear.

Trouble had begun a few months before Andy passed. He started taking Accutane, which is a prescription drug frequently prescribed for the treatment of acne. As a growing, hormonal young man, Andy had been struggling with acne for a couple of years. We sought treatment from our dermatologist, trying a variety of topical ointments and prescriptions, but nothing was ever effective. One day, Andy came home excited to tell me that some of the other boys at school had been taking Accutane with great success.

So, at our next appointment with the dermatologist, we asked him about this miracle drug and he told us that there may be side effects, but they were "minimal." The two areas of concern that he mentioned were its impact on bone density and liver function. The bone density wasn't really concerning to him as Andy was an avid milk drinker and clearly had a very strong bone structure. As for the liver function, he said he would test Andy's blood once a month to detect any possible changes.

Andy was super excited by the thought of finally getting rid of his acne, which was not only irritating, but a source of embarrassment. We decided to go ahead with the treatment. The doctor handed me a liability waiver for my signature, which I signed without reservation. It was not until about a month after Andy passed and the dermatologist called me, that I remembered seeing a couple of lines in small print that proclaimed (albeit quietly) that "suicide, psychosis, and depression are potential side effects."

Each month when Andy went back to the dermatologist, he had to first spend a bit of time talking to the doctor about how he felt and reporting if he was experiencing anything out of the ordinary. In short, it was a mini counseling session each month to evaluate Andy's state of mind at the time. In addition, the doctor also ordered blood draws to determine Andy's liver function, as well as to check for any other potential side effects or problems.

We went home after each appointment feeling excited that this wonder drug was having tremendous success eradicating my teenage son's acne.

Many people who have experienced the suicide of a loved one will swear that there weren't any signs at all. Nothing they missed, even in hindsight. This was true for Andy, as well, to a large extent. Honestly, though, in retrospect, I can see a few small signs, but nothing overtly telling. It wasn't like he was moping around depressed. He was generally a happy, funny kid and that rarely wavered. There were some minor changes in Andy's personality, but they could be easily dismissed as normal teenage angst. As much as I wish it weren't true, nothing really stopped me in my tracks or gave me any cause for concern.

There were times when Andy couldn't remember how to drive to certain baseball fields that we had been to dozens of times. He was also struggling with school a bit, which was something entirely new. Andy was not a big lover of school, but school had certainly never created problems for him in the past.

One night, when I was helping him study for a biology test, it seemed to me like he couldn't retain any of the content from his textbook no matter how many times we went over it. I got frustrated with him and said, "Andy, you really need to focus here, because your GPA is being affected by your apparent lack of concern." What I had no way of knowing then is that the drug was apparently affecting the functioning of his frontal lobe in his brain, where the clear-thinking process occurs. This part of the brain is one of the areas that is sometimes affected by the use of this dangerous drug.

There were other things going on, too, which helped to create the perfect storm where apparently suicide seemed the only remedy in Andy's mind. For anyone who might be feeling suicidal, I must be perfectly clear: Suicide is NOT the solution!

With help, Andy could have recovered from the side effects of the drug, as well as his perceived challenges and the pain in his heart. Sadly, the possibility of suicide for Andy— or anyone else, for that matter—was not on any of our radar screens. We hadn't ever known anyone who had passed by his or her own hand, and no one really talks about it anyway.

In 2012, when Andy relocated to Heaven, there weren't any suicide education, awareness, or prevention programs at school for the kids or their parents. This was uncharted territory for our family and apparently for Andy's friends, as well.

Even though I had signed the drug waiver, suing the dermatologist and the pharmaceutical company that manufactures Accutane was now part of what we were investigating with the attorneys. Had I not received that shocking call from Andy's doctor a couple weeks after our son passed, when he told me that he had reported to the FDA that Accutane had caused Andy's suicide, I probably wouldn't have made that connection in this terrible tragedy. Of course, I felt so disgustingly negligent on my part, as Andy's mom, for not having understood the reality of possible side effects from this awful drug. I talk openly about this whenever I speak because preventing all who will listen from ever taking Accutane is ranked near the top of my priority list.

The third possibility for legal action was against Andy's school, which was considered a closed campus. What exactly does that even mean? In this situation, the campus was gated, and all students had to pass through a guarded exit before leaving school. If they were planning to leave early, students first had to go to the office and get a permission slip reflecting a parent's or guardian's approval, which they'd then have to hand to the guard before leaving.

On Tuesday, December 11, 2012, Andy had gone to school just like he had any other day. His second hour was language arts, where journal writing was a daily requirement. That morning he wrote:

My winter break, I am most excited for my Dad to come home for nine days and spend Christmas with us. One thing that I am dreading the most is how my grades end up before the break.

Andy's dad, my husband Clay, had been working in North Dakota on a long assignment and could only come home for a few days once every two or three months. As much as Clay loves his work, the kids and I missed having him with us at home, and we looked forward to our family reunions whenever we got them. We were thrilled that he'd be home for a long Christmas break, and we knew we'd be spending quality time together as a family. I hadn't realized, until I read that entry in Andy's journal a couple weeks later, just how much Andy needed to spend more time with his dad than he had been.

In my mind, this was a forward-thinking journal entry by Andy, with some obvious concern for his grades. Not very surprising to me, his only difficulty was with one class taught by one particular teacher, and I will always wonder what happened at the end of second bell that morning that would trigger Andy to up and leave school.

I learned later that after the end-of-class bell rang, Andy walked off the grounds of the "closed" campus without anyone stopping him. What happened to cause him to do something so drastic and out of character? Why didn't anyone stop him or question where he was going? Why, when they take attendance every hour, didn't they let me know that Andy wasn't in his third hour, like he was supposed to be? What is the point of a closed campus and taking attendance every hour if it is only about punishment and not also about protection? Don't we believe that when we drop our kids off at school, we are entrusting them into the hands and protection of their teachers and other staff?

So many questions remain that will never be answered. Andy had never been tardy and had certainly never left school without explicit permission, so this was definitely out of character for him. If I had been notified, it would have instantly raised a red flag and a lot of concern on my part. I would have had five whole hours—yes, five—to have located my precious son before he retreated into his bedroom all alone and ended his life. If only someone had called me, like they should have! If protocol had been followed, this whole tragedy might have been avoided.

The grueling attorney selection process continued. We felt overwhelmed and about to throw in the towel when we finally met with Attorney Number Seven. Thankfully, we were referred to this gift of a man by someone we trusted, and he gave us excellent and empathetic counseling, as well as sound advice. After a lengthy meeting, I spent a couple of weeks exploring all the potential legal ramifications and set up a time for us to come back for a follow-up meeting. We were told, and rightly so, that the purpose of this meeting would be to be tutored on what our journey might look like in the event we chose to move forward with litigation.

After sufficient discussion, we all came to the same conclusion—that legal action would not be beneficial for our family's collective mental well-being. Four months had already passed by the time of this final meeting and some minor healing had already begun. We had also begun laying the groundwork for our future foundation formed in Andy's honor. As I previously mentioned, I wasn't interested in being handed a check because my son died, but I did want to do whatever I could to prevent anyone else from going down the same fatal road that Accutane had taken Andy down.

It was during those first few months that I realized I could do far more good in the world by sharing as a public speaker what I had learned than I could by filing any lawsuit, no matter how strong the case was that we could have presented. I had already started to share this message through the telling of Andy's story at some of our local schools. In fact, I was pretty sure that a lawsuit would close the doors of opportunity for me rather than open them.

At the end of the meeting with our attorney, he shocked and amazed me by saying that he and his firm would be willing to assist us in any ways that we might find valuable. At that moment, I had no idea where or when I would ever need to request his assistance, but it wasn't long before we were all entwined for the long haul in a glorious, lifesaving endeavor.

The formation of Andy Hull's Sunshine Foundation began in its infancy that very day, and none of us had realized that conception had even occurred. This firm would, indeed, form and file all of the necessary paperwork for our foundation pro-bono, and our attorney would additionally become a board member, which he is to this present day (in 2019). Our attorney also connected us with another like-minded, generous law firm that would file all the paperwork for our trademarking and consult with us whenever needed. We have been privileged to hold our monthly board meetings in the firm's conference room, which has helped draw in many other professionals who sit on our foundation's board of directors.

As I write, I am reminded of exactly why my family and I decided not to pursue legal action. Reliving the beginnings of this story took me back to where I felt almost entirely surrounded by pain. Had I gotten entrenched in a lawsuit, I would have been held hostage to all the painful memories rather than being a free-flowing spirit bringing Andy's sunshine to the world.

Understanding that whatever we focus on is what we will become was of vital importance to our family if we were ever to experience real joy, love, and happiness.

19

THE BIRTHDAY BOY

Birthdays have always been a big deal in our family—very large celebrations involving lots of great friends, delicious food, and plenty of fun. I'm talking birthday events with game trucks, clowns, bands, and much more. I would plan for each child's birthday several months, if not years, in advance—especially if it was one of those special ones like becoming a teenager, turning sixteen, and then eighteen. Unfortunately, we never reached that milestone with Andy, but we did have one heck of a memorable celebration for his sixteenth birthday.

April 10, 2012, the big sixteen for Andy finally arrived, just eight short months before he would ultimately move to Heaven. I'm so glad we didn't know on that special day what lay ahead for all of us.

Springtime in Phoenix can be totally unpredictable. We never know whether spring has really arrived or if winter might make one last cold blast of an appearance. As Andy's big day approached, it became clear that we were going to be visited by Jack Frost one last time. Since swimming was to be the main event of this party, the cold would pose a few problems for all the kids. Plus, there were likely to be about one hundred or so teenagers at my house for the festive celebration. *What will I do with that many kids in the house if all the rain and cold weather show up as predicted?*

At the time, we lived out in the desert on an acre of property, so under normal circumstances there would be lots of room for everybody. The saving grace was that we had a humongous L-shaped back patio that would accommodate however many kids the inside of the house would not.

The temperature outside was fifty-five degrees... forty... thirty-five ... and still dropping. And torrential rain with high winds. That was the latest forecast announced on the news the morning of our big party. Time to move to Plan B.

Warm food? Check. Warm drinks? Check. Even on the patio these kids were going to freeze in these conditions, and Lord knows I didn't want them inside, at least not all at the same time. I needed to find heaters—and soon—as the festivities for this momentous occasion were set to get underway in just under two hours.

Andy reminded me that his girlfriend's family had several large, freestanding patio heaters and he thought perhaps we could borrow them. Andy made the call to Katie. Then he and Jared, a good buddy of his, took off in Andy's truck to get them.

About thirty minutes later, I headed out to the store to pick up the birthday cake and also some last-minute goodies. As I was driving down Carefree Highway, I happened to see some commotion in my peripheral vision on the opposite side of the road. I slowed down for a moment in order to get a better look at what was happening.

A big blue truck heading in the opposite direction had stopped, and two teenage-looking boys were frantically collecting the remains of something on the road behind them. *Oh no! Could it be? It couldn't!* But it was. I spun my car around so I could lend a hand—by helping my darling son and his friend gather the remnants of the patio heaters that had been blown off the back of his truck in the high winds.

To say that Andy was upset would be an understatement. As for me, I was busy calculating the cost of replacing them and contemplating how embarrassed I'd feel when I explained to Katie's parents what had happened. It had never crossed my mind, and apparently not Andy's either, to lay the heaters down rather than stand them upright to keep the wind from blowing them out of the truck in one fell swoop. At least the heaters didn't topple onto any cars or, worse yet, hit anybody as they came crashing onto the ground.

While I proceeded on to the store to pick up the rest of the necessary items, Andy and Jared collected what was left of the heaters and headed home to see if any of them were still intact enough to be workable. Fortunately, one of the large heaters was still functional, even though it looked like someone had taken a baseball bat to it in an attempt to destroy it.

Clay and I had some small space heaters of our own. When combined with the only remaining big one that worked, as well as heat that was emanating from all of the bodies inside the house, we all managed to stay warm and a great time was had by all. Wild and crazy teenagers, by what seemed like dozens, were practically everywhere we looked. Lots of hot chocolate and pizzas were consumed to warm up everyone's insides.

Once the rain had finally stopped, the kids moved outside and built a huge bonfire in our stone fire pit. Fortunately, we had thought to cover the wood with plastic in anticipation of the storm, so it was plenty dry when Clay went to light the fire. It wasn't long before the happy-go-lucky kids were roasting marshmallows and shooting all kinds of firecrackers into the sky.

All in all, Andy's sixteenth birthday was a very memorable and comical one, as birthdays go. One for the books for sure, and to always cherish—especially since this birthday would turn out to be the last for my Sunshine Andy.

The big F-150 Ford truck I've described as Andy's had originally belonged to Clay, and Clay decided to gift it to Andy for his sixteenth birthday. This made for a very happy young man. Andy had just one more wish for this momentous occasion: custom black rims to make his new vehicle look like a monster truck. "I mean, if that's not asking too much, Dad," Andy said, grinning.

We would have given Andy the sun, the moon and the stars if he'd asked, but all he really wanted was the rims.

The morning after the party, Clay, Andy and I drove over to the Discount Tire store not far from our home, where Andy picked out the coolest rims ever—massive hunks of masculine-looking black metal. Even though I'm now the proud driver of Andy's pickup, those fancy cool rims remain on "our" truck to this day.

I get a kick, sometimes, when I think about a line from a song made famous by country artist Lee Brice: *Yeah, sometimes I drive your truck.*

Yep, Andy, sometimes I drive your truck.

Andy the Scout

Our beautiful family "before"

First day of Freshman year. Colton, Andy, Noah

Jared and Andy the Easter "before"

Wake-boarding on Bartlett Lake

Katie and Andy

Andy and his truck

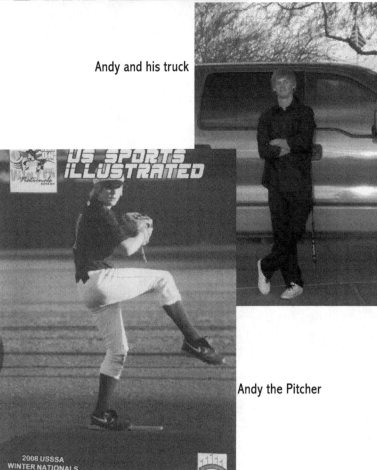

Andy the Pitcher

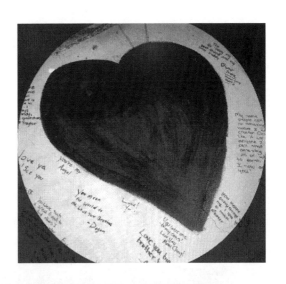

At the signing of the suicide prevention education bill
with Arizona Governor Jan Brewer (2014)

You Matter wristbands
making a difference

LeAnn speaking at one of many
schools about suicide prevention

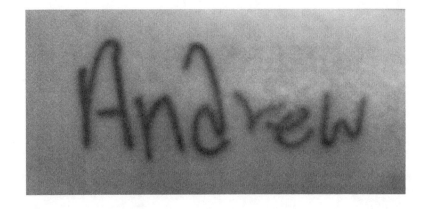

20

FIRST BIRTHDAY WITHOUT HIM

And just like that, the dreaded "first" of many more to come had arrived—the first birthday without our boy, our Sunshine Andy. Almost from the very first moments after Andy passed, I wondered what this day would be like and dreaded the very thought of it. I wondered how I'd ever survive.

It had been four short/long months since that horrible day. Time was like that now; it seemed to have a mind all its own. On one hand, I wondered how it could possibly be four months already, and on the other, time seemed to drag on and on. I found myself counting the seconds until I would be reunited with Andy in Heaven. In fact, my daily mantra for some time was "One day closer," and to be honest, sometimes it still is. What a terrible waste of life to be counting the days until we aren't here anymore, but that was the reality of my daily life at that point.

I told myself that we'd always celebrate the day of Andy's birth. It didn't matter whether he was here on the physical plane or not, because I knew he was always alive with me in Spirit. I made it a point to consciously count my blessings that Andy had been born, and that I had been privileged to be Mom to such a fine young boy, and then man, for sixteen wonderful years.

All of that was fine and dandy in theory but much more complex and difficult to swallow and follow through on. And then the big, daunting question: Who would show up to "celebrate" with me? Would people think I've lost touch with reality if I threw a party for my now-departed son?

Hesitantly, I posted my invite on Facebook. It looked like the weather was going to cooperate with us this year, and as it happened, we couldn't have asked God for better weather. It was a beautiful spring day, brimming with beauteous life that was being renewed and reborn.

Mesquite trees were sporting the vibrant, fresh, new green leaves that are truly of a distinct color and texture. The sky boasted wispy white clouds contouring the bluer-than-normal canvas due to it being a windy day—so typical during this time of year. Our own home-grown batch of quail eggs was hatching, too, and seeing the baby birds brought a smile to my face. I loved to watch the little quail families march around our property each day, looking for food and shelter.

We were lucky to have so many different types of animals and birds in our yard to keep us company. Besides the quail, resident owls were often heard hooting their way through the night, and several prowling coyotes marked their territory in our wash, or dry riverbed. Fierce, but blind, javelinas could be seen munching down on our various cacti. But my favorite of all had to be the many melodious cardinals who sang their glorious songs of faith, hope, and love. At least that's what they were for me. There was always something quite special about the cardinals and I believed they were speaking directly to me, to the depths of my very soul.

All around our property it was like Noah's Ark—two of everything, nature's perfect plan. Why couldn't things have been this perfect in my life? Why did our lives have to be suddenly so out of sync with nature? Though it didn't quite occur to me at the time, in nature there is always the cycle of life and death—and we were not an exception.

We wanted Andy's first heavenly birthday to be one that was fun for all the kids and would also provide some much-needed information on suicide awareness and prevention. Castles N' Coasters, an amusement park near where we lived in Phoenix, was always a place of great fun where people of all ages could find enjoyment and be entertained. I felt sure that what we needed was an event where advance discounted tickets could be sold, and we'd arrange for a variety of suicide prevention organizations to attend and hand out their valuable information to all the kids. Maybe a bake sale to add to the fun, too. *Did I hear someone say T-shirt sale?* Wow, I thought, *this could really be awesome!* Well, as awesome as anything could be at this moment of our continuing grief. I knew we'd need a handful of volunteers and someone in charge to make all of this come together. *Okay... I guess that person is me.* After all, I couldn't begin to imagine someone else planning my beautiful son's birthday. It *had* to be Mama, Mama Hull. It had to be me.

After making arrangements with Castles N' Coasters to purchase several hundred discounted tickets in advance, we were fully committed to this being The Party of the Year in all of Phoenix. I wanted to provide the kids with as many resources as possible for managing this most difficult challenge—this awful tragedy that would no doubt shape the rest of their lives.

But I also wanted the event to be really fun. All of us needed to realize that fun was not only possible, but necessary for us if we were to bring Andy forward with us as we went on with our lives. While I instinctively knew I'd be taking Andy with me as I got on with things, secretly I was walking in blind faith. I wasn't feeling this way inside at all... yet.

The tickets were selling like wildfire and everything fell into place quite easily. Many of the parents of Andy's friends volunteered to bake their favorite yummy deserts for our party. Bright sunshine yellow smiley face T-shirts had been donated by one of the baseball parents who owned a screen-printing shop. It quickly became evident that after all was said and done, a surplus of funds would be left over. Not only were people buying tickets, goodies, and T-shirts, but they were also donating money in Andy's memory.

The money came pouring in and it seemed like it never stopped. By the end of the evening, we had raised $10,000, even after all our expenses. My family and I quickly decided that the money would be used for the promotion of suicide awareness and prevention, and that's how Andy Hull's Sunshine Foundation was formed.

Love had risen up from the ashes of unbelievable sorrow and great loss—as had the infamous phoenix bird. This love—the love we all had for our Andy—was surrounding us, shrouding us from all the pain until we could see the light of day, once again.

On the morning of Andy's big party, a highly regarded tattoo artist came to our house. Andy's three siblings and several of his close friends—and I—had all decided to get the exact same tattoo in memory of our boy Andy. After much deliberation, we finally came to a unanimous decision: we'd each have a tattoo of "Andrew," written in his own handwriting—which we lifted right off of one of his homework papers. A better use of homework there never was!

Each of us decided on a different location on our bodies to place these energizing and artful memorials. I chose the inside of my left forearm, so that I would see my beautiful tattoo from the moment I first awaken until the welcome reprieve of sleep that accompanies me almost every night.

I also wanted others to see my body art and be curious, so that I could talk about my amazing kid wherever I went. And boy, did I. I was never afraid to talk about Andy with anyone; not at all ashamed of the way that he died, either. I simply needed to share my Andy with anyone and everyone who would listen—and I desperately wanted others to know how fully he had lived. Talking about Andy—and eventually with Andy—has helped me keep him alive in my heart and mind.

It was dusk when our party was ending, and none of us who had participated in the community "inking" wanted to part ways. After reflecting on what a fabulous day it had been, a dozen or more of our close family and friends stood strong together—some of us with plastic wrap still neatly wrapped around our fresh tattoos. We locked arms and gazed up into the night sky, hoping to catch a glimpse of some kind of sign from Andy in Heaven that all was well with him and with the world.

Suddenly, out of the corner of our eyes and toward the west, we saw it. Low on the horizon, the most brilliant blue comet, or star, or whatever it happened to be, came blazing across the sky in brilliant glory. It was precisely like Andy's blue spirit that had hovered over Clay and me in our bedroom that first morning after he transitioned—only this spirit was even more magnificent.

I couldn't have asked for a more perfect end to our evening, under the circumstances. I'm sure Andy was showing us his approval of all the hard work and love that had gone into making this night so spectacular.

Raising my eyes up to the night skies, I exclaimed, "Thank you, Andy, and Happy Birthday!"

Kyle Lewis

~

DRIFTKING
19

28-7-00
~
30-7-16

21

COPING

After living in North Dakota and later Wyoming for his employment, Clay's work eventually landed him south of Houston, near the gulf coast. As our busy schedules allow, we spend as much time together as we can—either in Phoenix, or wherever Clay happens to be working. Since Clay relocated to Texas in 2016, I have found great solace in spending time there, near the shore.

Sometimes, when my mood seems like a reflection of the overcast skies, I go down to Galveston beach about thirty minutes from Clay's home and sit at the water's edge. Watching the continuous waves rolling in and out helps me feel connected to something much, much bigger than even I can fathom. I like that. I need that. I choose to believe in a Higher Power that always, without exception, has my very best interests at heart—and shows me so. It reaffirms my faith and trust in God.

Rough seas reflect, to me, the volatility and fluidity of life—my life, at this time. Yet even as the waves crash onto the beach, I sense them seeking solace and rest, just as I do.

Where can you go to find that? Maybe you don't know how or where to look because your life seems too overwhelming.

I get that, and I hear that from a lot of people who are in pain and still struggling because of their recent losses. In fact, I have heard that so much lately from grievers that I'm beginning to think I'm abnormal because I do know how to help myself. Maybe I'm different, but I would much rather be this way than stuck in an isolating life pattern without any hope. I have always been a trailblazer, not a follower, but that sometimes comes with a hefty price.

Six years after Andy moved, I was asked to lead an online support group for parents who have lost children by suicide. It has been challenging, to say the least. I was hesitant to facilitate this group because I believe that this type of group can tend to offer up another form of isolationism and hammers home more deeply our sense of loss.

Some of the most common statements I've heard while leading this online group:

You don't understand my pain.

If you haven't lost a child, then you can't possibly know what I'm going through.

Losing a child to suicide is the worst.

No, it's much worse for me because my son was murdered.

On and on the comparisons go, but they never really accomplish a thing. Even within our small group at Helping Parents Heal, there have been comparisons to the various degrees of loss:

Well, my daughter was my only child and therefore it's worse.

No, my spouse doesn't support me, so I am all alone in this journey, which is much worse.

I think I have heard it all.

God forbid I post anything positive or uplifting on our closed group's Facebook page. Since the group is focused on moving forward after losing a loved one to suicide, wouldn't you expect to find and/or get some encouragement on this site?

No. Recently, I was verbally crucified for expressing my observation that we can choose our responses to loss. One mom actually told me that she had no choice in how she feels about losing her child and that I was being judgmental about how she was processing her pain. I wasn't being judgmental. I was simply giving options the group members might not have known about and offering up suggestions as to possible ways to maneuver their way through the grief. It's a help group, so wouldn't you expect some help to be offered?

One doesn't have to lose a child to understand deep pain and heartache. I have some very dear friends who have also faced difficult challenges: divorces, their own major illnesses, or losing spouses to cancer. I know they feel every bit as devastated about their losses as I do mine. The degree to which we feel pain is, in my experience, relative to their individual exposure to losses and their experiences with them.

We all have the ability to choose how we'll respond to our circumstances.

Will we choose anger? Stay depressed? Will we blame God for our loss or someone else? Can we ever have fun again? Find joy one day again and return to love? Will we have an amazing life? These are just a few of the questions that I believe we should be asking ourselves.

In my opinion, our society has been sold a big old bag of grief crap. We're told that there are appropriate stages of grief and loss that we must go through in order to be happy and healthy again. That will be another $300 and yes, please set up another appointment to process your process.

Forgive me if I sound a bit cynical. I'm aware that counseling is helpful for many people, but I've learned that it's not the best route to healing for everyone. I believe that the wrong counselor can do more harm than good. In fact, a bereaved mom recently told me that anger is something that you must go through in order to process grief. She believes this wholeheartedly because her counselor said it was true. This same woman concluded that my pain must not be as bad as hers since I never experienced anger to the degree that she has.

Let me be perfectly clear. When I'm speaking about anger, or sadness, or depression, I am talking mainly about a state of mind; not a situational momentary experience. Of course, I have felt anger. Later, I realized that reading her post is what made me so angry in the first place, about a number of things. But I am in charge of what I do with my emotions—including the emotion of anger.

I can choose to let anger become all-consuming and mess with my serene state of mind, or I can be proactive and work toward a solution of letting my anger go. After I kindly suggested that to her, she became very angry with me. This exemplifies my theory that some people just want to stay mad or blame someone else for all their problems and pain. Somehow that must seem easier to them than to fight, like I have, to be where I am today.

You might recall that in a prior chapter I referenced the famous quote by Dylan Thomas "I will not go gently into that good night!" This is a choice. Having a fulfilling, joyful, fun, and love-filled life takes hard work, and lots of it. Are you up for the task? Will you continue reading? Or will you throw this book away and tell me that I don't understand your pain?

22

THE PERFECT STORM

So, how did this happen to my Andy? As near as I can tell, there wasn't any one thing that led him to take his own life. I'm just surmising, though, since Andy isn't here to tell me and did not leave a note. It has been such a painful process, trying to piece together all the possible triggers that created this perfectly horrible storm; the one that Andy apparently thought was a little more than he could bear. I only backtrack now in an attempt to get a handle on what happened right under our noses and learn from it.

My family continues to reach out to assist others in finding hope and help by showing them how to make healthy choices. This has been our goal since Andy's move to Heaven. I know we will never fully understand why Andy left, but I hope that we'd at least be able to shine a light onto whatever led up to this tragic moment. Equipped with that information, we can then at least talk about the emotional triggers while offering others some possible coping skills that could be of benefit to them.

Let's begin with the effect that the Accutane had on Andy's brain. I believe this is where it all started—his ability to process the normal challenges of daily living was adversely affected. From my perspective, I noticed loss of memory and an inability to retain information, as well as some atypical displays of frustration and anger.

Had the dermatologist not connected those dots for me, I wouldn't have made the connection between this drug and Andy's suicide. It was certainly not obvious to me. But there were other possible triggers that may also have played a part in Andy's actions. Strange as it may sound, I have come to think of these triggers as learning tools. They are designed to help me and others be more thoughtful and compassionate in our everyday communications. At any given moment, we never really know what someone else's state of mind may be. What is it that lies behind the mask that every person wears every day? What is going on in their home lives or work lives that is coloring their emotional responses? Something that may seem insignificant to us might be a deadly emotional trigger that someone else cannot handle—such as a breakup, a failing grade in class, or a bad performance in a game.

Relationships seem to be at the heart of many suicides, and Andy was certainly struggling with one in the months leading up to his passing. That said, I am not blaming anyone here and do not hold this beautiful young woman responsible for Andy's choices. I hate even using that word "choice" because I honestly believe that the drug had impacted his thinking process so greatly that making a clear and healthy choice was not really possible for him on the day he died.

Andy and Katie had been very close to each other since they were in fifth or sixth grade. They attended winter and summer church camp together each year, as well as their many youth group activities. As the amount of time they spent together grew, so did their affection for each other.

When Andy wasn't playing baseball, he was over at Katie's house where they were swimming, eating, making funny videos, and just enjoying sharing their lives together. Her family had, for all intents and purposes, adopted Andy. They seemed to love having him around every bit as much as Katie. Everybody adored Andy, and he fit right in wherever he went. As close as Andy and I were, even I didn't know the extent of all the affection that so many people had for him until shortly after he had passed. He was Sunshine for all of us.

As time went on, Katie's family and ours began sharing some holidays, which we really enjoyed, and Andy was often invited on their family ski vacations and to visit their hometown of Bemidji, Minnesota. We easily melded together because of the deep love these two kids had for each other. Our family loved Katie, too, so this relationship had the approval of all parties.

By the spring of Andy's sophomore year, pressure had begun mounting on many fronts. Juggling, metaphorically, had become his new profession, and it was wearing on him. A serious relationship takes time to nurture and grow, and that can sometimes be too much for a busy teenager to handle. Andy was trying to keep all the balls of his various commitments in the air, but one by one they began to drop, and he knew he needed to make some adjustments.

Besides this intense relationship with Katie, Andy was also one step away from becoming an Eagle Scout, which placed many demands on his time. Baseball wasn't a casual activity for him, either. Andy was playing on the varsity team at school, along with club ball, which required the boys to have a lot of out-of-state travel.

Sports these days are so different from when I was a kid. We played some sports in the fall and others in the spring, but now practically every sport is a year-round endeavor. Even varsity baseball requires a year-round commitment, practicing and playing all through the summer—even after the season ends—as well as on every holiday. And if you're any good, add in club ball, and you are playing a lot of ball.

On any given weekend, these teams would play up to as many as eight games. Some tournaments lasted a whole week, like Winter Nationals. To say that this schedule was demanding is an understatement. To top it off, as the kids progressed in their abilities and got closer to the end of their high school years, the baseball scouts began to show up and follow every little thing the kids were doing. In the case of a prized left-handed pitcher like Andy, they were constantly checking on his earned run average (ERA), as well as his school grade point average (GPA).

Getting a college scholarship or being recruited to play professionally was a dream come true for most boys and was definitely at the heart of everything Andy did. He loved baseball with all his heart and wanted very much to play professionally.

The reason the baseball scouts were constantly checking on the GPAs of their prospects was because they did not want to make a bad investment on behalf of their schools or franchises. They wanted to make sure they were only offering college scholarships to boys who would give them a lot of bang for their buck. Grades always needed to stay consistent, and Andy's were—that is, until he came up against one particular teacher.

Some teachers don't appreciate good humor and actually seem repulsed by students who are fun-loving and happy people. Often, it's the student whom everyone else adores. The woman who taught Andy during his second hour was one such instructor. Andy was funny and goofy, and she made it clear that she did not appreciate this about him whatsoever. Try as Andy might to change this, they remained like oil and water. Their personality conflict was soon reflected in Andy's poor grades.

Truth be told, there wasn't anything he was doing academically that should have resulted in the failing grade she was giving him. To make sure I wasn't being a biased mom, I began thoroughly reviewing Andy's homework and helping him study, and I concluded—along with Andy—that she was indeed bullying and punishing him for his gregarious and funny disposition.

All of Andy's other teachers loved him. His grades in every other class were in perfect alignment with the effort he had always applied to his work. Unfortunately, though, this one teacher in this one class had the ability to block any potential scholarship opportunities, and managed to make Andy ineligible to play varsity baseball.

When this all began to unfold, I urgently reached out to Andy's teacher. When I received a strong negative response, I moved on to the head of the language arts department, who sided with the teacher. Furious, I made my way to Andy's counselor and the dean of students, complaining that Andy was being unjustly bullied by this one instructor.

It didn't help. Like the others, the counselor and dean sided with the teacher and did not consider the fact that Andy wasn't having any trouble with other teachers, or in any other class at all. This is a problem, not only in schools, but in society at large. Too often, adults side with adults when they shouldn't, and kids' lives are way too frequently put in jeopardy.

Funny, if you interfere too much for your kid, then you're considered a helicopter parent (one who constantly hovers) but if your kid completes suicide, then people rush to ask, "What the heck did you miss?" and "Why didn't you see this coming?" Welcome to my world, and sadly, that of many other parents just like me.

Finding time for his friends, girlfriend, family, the Scouts, schoolwork and church was more than Andy could juggle, so something would have to give. I'm not sure there are many people who could have managed all that was on Andy's plate, and at such a young age. Unfortunately, in trying to sort out his priorities, he made a choice regarding Katie that he would soon come to regret, and which caused him very deep pain and heartache.

In his teenage boy mind, Andy thought he could just slow things down with her and that she would understand why and be fine with that. Needless to say, Katie was not a bit happy about his decision, and they wound up breaking up altogether.

Their relationship had been so deep and serious that, even at sixteen years old, they had already talked about wanting marriage and children together one day, and felt they were making long-term plans for a future together.

With that level of intensity, the severing of their union caused deep and gaping wounds for both of them. I knew they still loved each other, and I was confident they would find their way back into each other's arms and hearts when the timing was right. But young people don't often possess that same kind of long-term thinking. Everything is immediate and urgent. Most can't think much past the next hour. Consequently, everything for them is a tragedy that results in the end of the world.

As summer progressed, Andy and Katie both found other people to date. While I felt certain they were distracting themselves with other people, they were still communicating to a certain extent. Andy soon came to regret his decision and asked for Katie to come back.

I don't think Katie was in love with this other young man. Rather, her heart was broken, and I suspect she wanted to punish Andy for the pain he had caused her. As it's been said, *hell hath no fury like a woman scorned.* I tried to convince Andy that she was just hurt and was lashing out at him in retaliation. I told him I was confident that Katie would eventually find her way back to him if he could just be patient. Teenagers and patience, what an oxymoron. Andy was quite mad at himself for losing her. He was so distraught, there wasn't any talking to him, from anyone, that really helped.

During what would ultimately be the last week of Andy's life, I could feel the pain in his heart about his lost relationship. By this time, it had become nearly all-consuming for him. Katie and Andy had planned to meet for coffee on a Friday, and in an attempt to win Katie back and express his deep feelings of regret, Andy wrote her a beautiful and tender love letter that he wanted to give her before they met. Hoping to get my input on this labor of love prior to e-mailing it to her, Andy asked me to look it over and tell him my honest thoughts.

This was a love letter that any woman, be they sixteen or sixty, would be thrilled to receive. After hearing my beaming approval, Andy e-mailed his heartfelt letter to the love of his life and hoped for the best. He was so excited to have made plans to meet with Katie that he stopped by my work to tell me. Then off he went, feeling so hopeful, and I'm sure with his heart beating wildly in anticipation.

I am thankful his buddy, Degan, went with him for moral support in case things didn't go as Andy hoped. Neither Andy nor Degan saw what was coming and certainly didn't understand the impact it would have on my son's brain and his tender heart.

Unfortunately, that Friday meeting didn't go the way Andy had wanted. Katie did not want to get back together, which was hard for him to hear. Then, to make matters worse, other kids in the coffeeshop who overheard the conversation began to heckle my son. All of this, coupled with so many other mounting pressures with school and all his other commitments, led Andy to feel hopeless and in great distress. This bullying, as I later learned, turned out to be the last straw for my poor son and sent him spiraling further downward.

Andy had not shared with me his disastrous encounter at the coffee shop. I think he was in such shock that he had to completely shut himself down. He was still functioning, but he'd apparently given up on hope and, ultimately, life.

The next evening, as we were driving back from an Eagle Scout ceremony, Andy casually said to me in an uplifting tone... "Mom, if I go before you, I want it to be a celebration."

The Scout event had been fairly religious, so in my mind he was simply expressing his deep faith and belief in an afterlife in Heaven with God. I didn't hear the goodbye in his words, but now I'm sure that's exactly what he was saying. Andy didn't seem very distressed or sad when he said that, so I thought nothing of it at the time. It's only by benefit of hindsight that I can clearly see that that was Andy's goodbye.

Tuesday morning arrived like any other day, and off to school Andy went. Before he left, we had discussed his grades and the steps that would be necessary for him to be eligible for varsity ball. I thought Andy understood that I was working on managing this problem with his teacher, but apparently, he hadn't believed it or internalized it in any real way.

I've asked myself a million times, what happened during second hour that morning that pushed Andy so far over the edge? I don't know for certain, but I can only surmise that his teacher told him she was going to fail him.

Andy walked out to his truck, left the school campus, and was missing in action for five hours before ultimately heading home. Once there, he watched a horrible music video that, as police detectives later revealed to me, mimicked the last half-day of Andy's life on Earth to a tee. Most of it was too dark and dangerous to be repeated here. Suffice it to say, the perfect storm had arrived and left unbelievable devastation in its wake.

Charlie

Created with L♥VE - Mom, Sam,
Reiley, Brady, Lauren, Kenny

To infinity...
and
beyond...

23

THE SIGNED BASEBALL

And just like that, the first baseball season without Andy was ending. Sad as I felt inside, I had made my way to the baseball diamond—for the home games and the away—thirty-three times, without my beautiful boy. I pulled up in his truck, got out, and with my feet being propelled by some unforeseen force, I climbed up the stands and sat down on the hard metal bleachers. Whenever the score was tied, I paced back and forth; cheered each time another awesome play had been made; and at the end of every game I walked, alone and silent, back to Andy's truck and drove home.

With each game came a new awareness of a strength that even I never knew I had. What is it that pushes us through such unimaginable pain? Masochism of some form? Was it punishment for not having protected my child?

No! It was love and only love. Love moves us forward when nothing else will. Anthony Robbins hit the nail on the head, for me, when he said:

"I believe life is constantly testing us for our level of commitment, and life's greatest rewards are reserved for those who demonstrate a never-ending commitment to act until they achieve. This level of resolve can move mountains, but it must be constant and consistent. As simplistic as this may sound, it is still the common denominator separating those who live their dreams from those who live in regret."

I knew deep down in my heart that if I persevered, my actions would eventually transform my pain into love.

Did it get easier as time went on? Was the old adage, 'Time heals all wounds' really true? Maybe in certain circumstances it is, but for me and the loss of my child, I can honestly say that I have simply learned to live a little better with my new reality. I have used the pain to open my heart and see the world and the people in it in a different light. When faced with a devastating experience, we really only have two choices: Love and acceptance, or anger and bitterness. Well, perhaps there's also a third. We might also allow ourselves to be lost in numbness, nothingness, and emptiness; a life devoid of any meaning or purpose.

I was thinking recently about the choices I make today in my life since Andy's move. Just then, a song by King and Country came over the radio—"Joy"—with the refrain of "And I choose joy." That is not a coincidence. When we learn to tune into what is actually going on all around us, it's easy to see there really are no coincidences in life. In fact, I like to think that coincidences are God's way of letting us know He is with us. Yes, I choose joy—pure, unadulterated joy. It's up to me how I live my life each day, and what I choose to fill it with. My life is infinitely better because I choose joy.

Don't get me wrong, there are still times when the loss of Andy will drop me to my knees in excruciating anguish and gut-wrenching cries, but time has softened each occurrence and they come now with much less frequency. Most of the time I really don't feel that ache in my heart and belly that I used to, but it has taken a lot of work and effort on my part to vigilantly manage my own mental health.

I also understand that some people are not capable of doing this on their own and will have better success with the help of a mental health professional. Remember, there is no right or wrong way of taking care of yourself, just healthy or unhealthy choices. Get to know yourself before a tragedy occurs so that you can be your own best advocate when or if tragedy strikes.

The baseball championship game had arrived, with this outstanding varsity team's record of twenty-nine wins and four losses. Several other teams in our division had been pegged for the record that these boys had, but after Andy left, these young men had found a purpose fueled with a passion that gave them an extra edge in every game. They were driven to win this season for their friend who was still with them, but no longer physically present. Without a doubt, Andy was there at every game. He had imprinted his love for the game on their hearts, and it had translated into an unbelievable season.

All sorts of reporters, scouts, and our entire community had become intrigued by this unexpected and unusual winning season for the Sandra Day O'Connor Eagles. The team had always done well, but nothing quite like this. With each game, more and more people showed up to witness this triumphant effort. News stories were being written at every turn, and this season would go down in the history books as a heartwarming classic.

It was always every player's dream to be written about in the newspaper or to have some scout want to talk with him about his future baseball plans. I was always such a players' enthusiast that I saved all the articles about Andy and his teams' accomplishments since T-ball. Odd as it may sound, these boys seemed oblivious to all the attention they were garnering during this season.

Their hearts had been wounded so deeply that no amount of recognition would fix that. They seemed to understand they were being healed through the process of doing. They were playing their way to a place where they could have Andy present with them, and in a manner that did not crush their spirits.

They also knew, in their heart of hearts, what it took for me to show up at every game and were determined to offer me their best in every single thing they did. I could feel the warmth of their love in every catch they made, in every at-bat they took, and in every win that they snagged. Little by little, much like a patchwork quilt, my heart was being pieced back together. I have never felt such pure love—before or after—from anyone, let alone seventeen- and eighteen-year-old boys.

The first championship game had gone into extra innings due to a tie score, and tensions were mounting high. I found myself climbing, literally, on the chain-link fence and cheering with every play, along with all the other proud parents.

Then the final moment arrived. The last inning was here. The final pitch thrown. The final out made. We won! Although they were mixed with sorrow, we cried sweet tears of joy and relief at a job very well done. All of us won that day.

As I looked around at all the people who had come to witness this moment, I saw that everyone had something to do and someone with whom to share. Everyone, that is, but me. I knew that the boys would want to be interviewed by the reporters and various scouts. This was their moment of glory.

But they didn't come off the field right away. I watched them huddle on the pitching mound for what seemed like an eternity, and then they began to make their way in a line toward the gate where I was standing. *What in the world are they doing? What's taking them so long?* After all, this was their proudest moment.

Then one by one, each of those friends of Andy walked off the field and came straight to me. With their sweaty arms wrapped around me, they said, "We did this for Andy and you."

As I would soon come to realize, the extra time out on the pitching mound was because all the boys were autographing the winning ball. At the end of their procession, they ceremoniously presented it to me as a tribute to their deep love for their Sunshine friend. This precious baseball is proudly displayed in a trophy case in our home, sealed at the perfect pressure to preserve all the treasured signatures.

Out of deep pain and trauma are born deep healing and love. The boys and I learned this lesson together throughout the course of that season. Without this tragedy, I doubt any of us would have discovered just what we were made of—especially to the extent that we did. I'm sure that if given the choice, every one of us would have Andy back in a heartbeat—even if it meant taking a lifetime to learn all these valuable lessons.

But the gift in the wound of this unbelievable loss is that we found, within ourselves, the ability to love deeply, on a magical and transformative level. Holding the baseball tight to my chest, I once again made my way down the long and lonely sidewalk back to Andy's truck. Just as I began to sense a familiar arm wrapped around my shoulder, I heard my Andy softly say, *I'm so proud of you, Mom.*

24

YOU MATTER

Andy's junior year had started with such hope and promise and ended with a pall of sadness hanging over all of us. Anticipation of summer vacations and out-of-state baseball tournaments had vanished into thin air. Sometimes I would try to trick my mind into believing that Andy was simply away at school and that one day he would be back. But that just wasn't the case.

The finality of death is unlike anything we will ever encounter in life. No amount of time, money, patience... nothing fixes death. It exists in a category all its own and feels as if it has a life all its own, too. Allowing Andy's death to merge with my life taught me how to harness the power it had over me in the beginning of my grief journey and learn to control it.

At first, I did not even realize I was doing this, but I used the energy from this merger to breathe life back into my life. Each time I talked about Andy with anyone and shared how he'd moved to Heaven, I gained a little more strength and courage to face whatever might lie ahead. The same was true whenever I showed up at events in support of his friends. I never shied away from a discussion about Andy, suicide, or death. I owned this journey and was determined to not let it define me but rather to use it as a tool to help me grow and change into the warrior woman awakening inside me.

There were many occasions during which I put my journey through loss and pain to good use. One involved my decision to put all the money that we had raised at Andy's Heavenly Birthday Party at Castles N' Coasters toward a meaningful purpose. If I jumped on it right away, I knew just the perfect one. Every year, most schools have an award assembly where college scholarships are handed out to the graduating seniors and I desperately wanted to be a part of the upcoming one at Andy's high school.

A group of us had already been working on forming what would soon become the board of directors of Andy Hull's Sunshine Foundation. Of the $10,000 we raised at the party, we agreed to award ten $1,000 scholarships to graduating seniors who completed a "You Matter" essay that we'd create. Collectively, we decided what the essay should be composed of, and what the goal of writing such an essay would be.

We asked the students to describe who they mattered to and why, as well as to write about what might be their own personal contribution to the grand scheme of life. We had also decided that we didn't want the potential recipients to be limited by their GPA, since this was not an academic scholarship, but rather one that recognized them for the depth of their thought processes. Our only requirement was that they must be planning on attending college or a technical school and that the money was specifically to be used for payment toward those expenses.

The question we posed regarding their personal significance to someone seems to be something that most people struggle with at one time or another. Is it enough to just exist, or do we have to do or accomplish something extraordinary?

Do we need to win the Nobel Peace Prize? Or is it enough to go through life with no or seemingly few perceived accomplishments that are visible to others?

For some reason, being busy usually translates into feelings of self-importance and self-worth. That's why retirement is so hard for most folks. We may feel that we have lost our value in society and thus feel that we don't matter. So, do we matter because of what we are doing or is it enough just to exist? That famous quote by William Shakespeare, "To be or not to be, that is the question," provides us with an opportunity to examine the meaning of life. Each individual needs to define this for himself or herself because it is certainly a worthy point to ponder.

Though our nonprofit was not yet officially formed, we managed to get Andy Hull's Sunshine Foundation listed on the program for The Senior Awards and Scholarships Ceremony as one of the organizations that would be awarding scholarships on this special evening. There seemed to be a mysterious, magical force working behind the scenes to open doors in order to make things happen. My band of devoted friends and I were being guided toward something that none of us had even conceived of, much less imagined to be possible. If you think about it, most non-profits are founded because someone suffered a hardship and later used it to benefit either a specific group of people or society at large. Ours was yet to be really defined, but it was already on the move, touching people's lives as we journeyed forward, and that made me so happy.

After selecting a panel of judges to read the essays that had been collected, we began the process of selecting who the recipients would be for our scholarship money. It was truly uplifting and inspiring to get a glimpse into the hearts and minds of these young people who came from such diverse backgrounds.

Surprisingly, they all seemed to possess an understanding of what we were looking for, but time would tell whether they would actually be able to carry these concepts forward to assist them in their lives as they grew older. It is one thing to write about what someone is asking you to do, but quite another to implement those principles in a lifelong process of thinking. We were hoping that this task would help the kids learn how to dig deep into the depth of their souls, and also give them some additional tools that would come in handy when they faced some of the challenges that lay ahead.

When the awards evening arrived, it was another great opportunity for me to choose to own this journey. Every time I stepped onto that school campus after Andy's move, my heart skipped a beat and I felt like I couldn't breathe. My stomach would ball up into a tight knot of emotions and the pain of what was lost and what could have been felt overwhelming.

Every step I took that night reminded me that my process of "doing and moving" was inching me closer and closer to a place of renewed strength and control over my challenging life. Would I ever stop missing my son or wishing that he was here? Of course not. But over the next few years, I would eventually reach a place where love, joy, happiness, and fun superseded the all-consuming pain and anguish that I had first been experiencing in this new life without my Andy.

As I sat on that school stage, fragile but so very proud, I realized that life would indeed go on through the hopes and dreams of these other brave young adults. The legacy of my son, Andy "Sunshine" Hull, would be carried with them through their accomplishments and by the power of my choosing love over fear. Andy had laid the groundwork for me to deliver a life-sustaining message that had the potential both to change and to save lives.

When I stood to hand out the awards, I first spoke briefly about the origin of all these scholarships. Then I announced each recipient's name as I called them up to the stage to receive their well-deserved awards. The evening was so emotionally moving for me, it took me nearly two days to recover.

I had no idea that night how strong the correlation is between emotional recovery and physical well-being, but the days to follow would surely show me.

Anahi Gileen Ruiz

12/29/03   09/18/17

25

CANCER

Does one great tragedy preclude us from having another one arise in our lives? When we study the Bible or various history books, we can quickly see that horrific events often occur multiple times within one lifetime. I can say that, for myself, after having lost a child, I thought that nothing could be worse than what I had already experienced. Truly, it is every parent's biggest nightmare and worst fear realized.

I honestly believed that some universal karma would protect me from anything else terrible happening. That God would bestow upon my family His compassion and mercy and spare us from further anguish. Wasn't it enough for me to have to move forward without my Andy? Deep down, I knew that God is not some puppet-master sitting up on His throne choosing who will suffer and who will be spared. We live in the world and crap happens. God is our comforter, not some genie in a bottle with a magic lamp. At least this is how I believe the world works and, in some ways, this gives me comfort.

The word "cancer" is oftentimes synonymous with the word "death." It scares us to our very core. We wouldn't even wish it on our worst enemies. Unfortunately, though, six months after Andy moved to Heaven, that awful word became a part of our everyday vernacular. I've learned through some of my support groups that when one or more parents have experienced the death of a child, a greater possibility exists of experiencing a life-threatening illness or divorce.

It is quite easy to see how this would be possible. The devastating shock that the mind and body go through after a tragic event such as the loss of a child is nearly impossible to describe. While there are evidential medical terms that describe these physical and emotional processes that we experience, it's enough to say that nothing is working normally. The chemical makeup of our bodies changes, as well as our thoughts, and I'm surprised that anybody survives.

That proved to be true for us because, just like that, our world was turned upside down all over again.

What had begun as a tiny sore (the size of a small pea) on the top of Clay's head in early 2013 had, a few months later, suddenly grown into something much larger. During a routine checkup, Clay mentioned this spot to his doctor, and it instantly changed the trajectory of our lives and that of our family. The diagnosis was stage IV melanoma, a sometimes-fatal form of skin cancer. Another punch in the gut for all of us.

Fear of the unknown and the all-too-common ending of this type of diagnosis had left us in a state of shock and feeling panicked. Fortunately, though, shock serves quite a useful purpose in that it helps most people function—or at least it did for Clay and me. While this is not necessarily true for everyone, I'm thankful for our ability to think and make decisions, even in the darkest of times.

We were immediately directed toward the recommended path of treatment. For Clay, surgery, chemotherapy and radiation were looming large on the near horizon. According to the doctors, there are no other options, and they know best. Or, so they think.

Not only did the cancer present us with a serious challenge, but Clay had been working on assignments in other states for several years. Because life has to go on and bills still need to be paid, Clay had returned back to work in North Dakota one month after Andy moved. I, too, had returned to work at my job at about the same time.

Getting back into a routine was good for both of us, as it kept our minds occupied, at least for the time we were working. That doesn't mean that we didn't often fall apart. We did. In the beginning, this happened to both of us several times a day. I know this because even though we were living in different states, we always talked at least a half a dozen times every day. We helped keep each other pushing forward. Lord knows, we did not want to go backward.

In the past few years, I have seen far too many parents who have stayed at home way too long after their losses. While I certainly understand that after a tragedy we want to just crawl into a hole and cocoon, this can actually stifle the healing process. I know from first-hand experience how hard it can be to function. But every hour, every day, every month that we get up and put one foot in front of the other is one step closer to finding some sense of peace and joy.

This principle applies no matter what the nature of the loss that you have gone through. It could be a divorce, an infidelity, getting fired, or many other of life's common occurrences. At some point, you have to decide to push through no matter what, or risk getting stuck in your pain and grief and likely becoming bitter and angry.

Clay knew that during his rigorous treatment, he could not stay in North Dakota alone without help. He had no other choice but to pack up and come home. Fortunately, one of our friends offered Clay a job in Phoenix while he was undergoing treatment, which he gratefully accepted. Thankfully, the company Clay worked for in North Dakota kept him on their insurance for as long as we needed it. What a blessing!

Surgery was scheduled for June 2013, the week of Clay's return to Phoenix, and plans were being made for the follow-up treatment schedule. Looking back on this, I find it incredible just how quickly we can adapt to unforeseen obstacles when we have to. The brain is truly an amazing organ. Since our friends were still reeling from Andy's death, we chose not to tell most of them about what was happening with Clay, for fear they couldn't handle any more bad news. People are funny creatures. They can only handle so much pain for so long, so if you don't snap right back, poof, they vanish into thin air. We were already losing friends at the speed of sound and we couldn't bear the thought of losing any more.

Clay and I drove to the hospital the morning of his surgery, prepared for the worst but hopeful that the operation would eradicate all the cancer. Then we would be done with this horrible chapter. As a nurse came into Clay's room and wheeled him away, I said as many prayers as I could, but one in particular still stands out in my mind. I told God that I'd be extremely pissed off if Clay got to Heaven—and Andy—before me; therefore, Clay needed to be okay. Realizing that we were now in a competitive race to beat each other to Heaven was a startling and stark reality. It's not like we were eager to get there, but neither of us wanted to be left behind by the other.

After a couple of hours, when they finally allowed me back into the recovery room to see my poor husband, I began trembling at the sight of the gigantic bandage wrapped all around his head. Also, since they had taken skin from the top of his thigh to use for a skin graft, he had an additional open wound that needed to be treated. As the surgical wound was the size of a medium orange, the bandage on his head practically covered the entire top of his skull. Apparently, the cancer had spindled out quite a distance beneath the skin and so what looked tiny on the skin's surface was actually very large underneath.

As we were waiting for the doctors to arrive with the verdict, I'm sure Clay and I looked dazed and confused. With blank stares on our faces, we awaited the news of our fate.

It was not good. The look of gloom on the doctor's face said it all. With this type of cancer, he said, we'd need to report to Banner MD Anderson Cancer Center in Gilbert, Arizona, to begin chemo and radiation without delay. We drove home in relative silence, both numb.

Within the first week after surgery, the appointment for follow-up treatment had been scheduled. We were like blind sheep following the shepherd without any idea that there were any alternative treatments available. We were simply doing what the oncologist told us to do because that is what people do. We are so conditioned to not question the seemingly superior knowledge of the medical professionals that most of us, most times, don't even give our course of treatment a second thought.

So off we went to nearby Gilbert, to MD Anderson. As we sat in the conference room listening to the many different types of procedures and drugs that Clay would soon be receiving, something began stirring in both of us simultaneously. First, the list of drugs to counteract the effects of radiation and chemo: anti-depressants, anti-nausea medicine, sleeping aids, blood pressure meds, et cetera. On and on they went. Then the length and frequency of treatment: once a week for two years. I couldn't even imagine. Then the prognosis: with treatment, two years to live. And they would be miserable years from all the various procedures and drugs.

Clay and I looked at each other without any discussion and, almost in unison, said, "Nope, we're leaving. This treatment plan isn't for us."

If only we could have captured the look of astonishment on all of their faces. Yet, if you only have two years to live and the treatments are only going to make those years miserable, then why would you go through all the agony? What about quality of life? If there isn't a cure, then what's the point?

We walked out of the doctor's office that day and never looked back. Of course, they called us several times to inform us we were making a terrible mistake. Eventually, we just quit answering their phone calls.

Relief came over us first, then peace. We stared this cancer monkey in the face and took control over the rest of Clay's life, no matter how long that would be. Not only was death no longer something we feared, but there was no way in hell we were willing to add any more physical or mental suffering to our plates. If Clay had only two years left to live, then by God, we were going to live them. We didn't know how quite yet, but just like the rest of this amazing journey, the answers would soon appear.

26

A New Outlook

The summer months were mostly spent healing our minds and our bodies. While Clay and I had both returned to work two weeks after his surgery, we were definitely not operating at full capacity. Days came and went without fanfare. Every morning we'd open our eyes, hoping that the nightmare we were living was just that—a nightmare, and not really real. But reality would soon infiltrate through the fog in our brains and jolt us back to the exhausting job of discovering, once again, how to get through the day. Were we to exist like this or could we change and eliminate that ever-present gut ache that permeated our very souls? Somewhere down deep inside, I felt the stirring of hope. Was it a delusion or did my will to live supersede my desire to fade away?

Yes, our commitment would soon become clear: we both wanted to live, if only to preserve the memory and legacy of our cherished son.

Getting ready in the morning for each day quickly became a very important task. Preparation became one of the key ingredients to healing all of our wounds, both physical and emotional. We learned that healing the body actually begins with healing the mind. First and foremost, we needed to treat and care for Clay's physical wound, but how and why it occurred proved to be a question that required much more attention.

As previously mentioned, the potential for serious illness and/or other significant loss is indeed quite a bit higher after a traumatic event, and we surely had something terrible occur in our lives in the aftermath of Andy's passing. I reasoned that my body seemed free of illness because I was actively talking about Andy and processing my pain and grief through our soon-to-be foundation. I wasn't holding anything in, which allowed the grief energy to flow right out of my body.

Clay, on the other hand, wasn't talking about Andy or much of his pain at all. He had buried himself in his work and, because he was out of state most of the time, that was fairly easy for him to do. Clay missed Andy so much and was doing his very best to block out the anguish. The sad news is, though, that he kept it all buried inside of him. At some point, we have to release our pain, or it will manifest itself somewhere, in some other unproductive way.

Clay and I absolutely believe that his cancer was the manifestation of his deep, unexpressed grief. I'm not sure we really understood that at this stage in the journey, but from all of our business training, we understood first-hand the awesome power of our thoughts. As famed author and motivational speaker Zig Ziglar would say, we had some real "stinkin' thinkin'!" Clay and I knew that it was up to us, and nobody else, to change in order to make our physical and emotional states better. For us, step one would be to begin searching for the answers to better health, and we knew that we didn't have all of the tools necessary to accomplish this.

Clay began researching alternative treatments for cancer while I read books that altered my thought processes. These were books that helped me feel empowered and put me back into the driver's seat of this rugged road we were traversing. I knew that if those other inspirational people could overcome their trials and tribulations, then I could find my own way, too. I would pull bits and pieces from all the books that I read and ultimately create my own style and brand of deep healing.

Simultaneous with my having read eighty inspirational books, Clay's search led him to some great resources that gave him the tools necessary to become healthy and cancer-free. Now, six years after his death sentence, Clay is cancer-free, having had zero chemo or radiation. Did we know, back then, that it was possible? No. But we did come to know that the power of belief and hope is much stronger than the power of worry and fear. We just had to make the decision to get started—which is often the hardest part of any transformational journey.

We also learned that part of our preparation had to involve doing something physical every day. We became vigilant about avoiding the temptation to lie around the house all day feeling sorry for ourselves, or commiserating with each other about how awful our circumstances had become. Clay and I had to schedule daily outings to keep our minds and our bodies occupied. This type of busyness provided great relief to our brains which, in turn, gave our minds and our hearts time to heal.

We learned that when we are no longer consumed by pain, we slowly gain confidence that we can actually exist without it. Every minute, every hour, every day that we got through helped us to garner strength and faith that we would survive all these horrible life events. After a period of time, we began to have reference points to reflect back on, so we could measure our progress and feel encouraged.

Hopefully, the older we get, the greater our ability becomes to understand that "This, too, shall pass." Time will soften the pain if we put a good, workable plan of action into place—and "act" is the keyword in this equation.

After Andy moved, the tasks that used to be simple enough to accomplish had suddenly become, for me, quite exhausting and challenging. Activities like grocery shopping, going to the bank, and picking the kids up from school were just some of the everyday things that Clay and I were both trying to maneuver our way through. Because thinking had now become a task in and of itself, it felt like the circuitry in our brains had been rewired or rearranged.

My favorite saying used to be that "my train left the station without me and we'll just have to wait a bit for it to return." I'd start a sentence, and before I could even finish it, I would forget what I was even saying.

These are just some of the effects of PTSD, which everyone in our family was now displaying to varying degrees. Forgetfulness was another symptom of our trauma. Writing out to-do lists was an essential part of making sure things got done. Even reading was tough. We all struggled with reading even one paragraph, and then if we actually read it, we couldn't remember for more than two seconds what it had said. As such, I would have to read and re-read several times most of the sentences in order to retain information. Equally as challenging as staying on any task was beginning to do it. In the early months of my grief, I'd never have been able to write this book, not even one chapter.

We also discovered that if we were going to move forward, patience with ourselves and others was critical. Our society has become so accustomed to instant gratification that if we don't get or achieve what we want immediately, then we usually give up on it altogether. A perfect example of this is our phones. If our phones aren't fast enough or don't offer the newest and greatest technology, we instantly want new ones. Likewise, if our marriages are unfulfilling, we are told over and over by our friends and media that we deserve better and should opt out of our marital contracts and search for new and improved partners.

Patience and persistence with ourselves have become some of our essential tools that we have used over and over again on this journey. Failure was never an option since we had other children and grandchildren who loved and needed us. We had to persevere and do the hard work of fixing ourselves. These kids did not deserve broken parents or grandparents, literally or metaphorically. Our kids should not have to worry about how we are every time they walk through our front door. Much to the contrary. We encouraged them to always feel free to come bursting into the house whenever they wished and, with all the gusto in the world, to share with Clay and me whatever wonderful things they were experiencing in their young lives.

Kindness and gentleness were virtues that we needed to instill in ourselves as well as others. Reinventing ourselves and our lives was not going to be easy. We knew that it would take lots of hard work and would probably wind up being something we would seek to improve upon for the rest of our lives.

Forgiving ourselves when we'd had a bad day, or felt like we took two giant steps backward, was something we'd often have to remind ourselves to do. We discovered that giving ourselves the gifts of plenty of rest and TLC became essential to a healthy mind and body. Nothing was set in concrete, though, and in addition to the way in which we decided to journey, we allowed ourselves the flexibility of time to get where we needed to be.

It was a dance of sorts, I suppose: two steps forward, one step back, and then side-to-side. The last thing any of us needed was more anxiety or judgment about how or why we were doing certain things in our lives. Clay and I had to show up to the dance, day after day, and keep practicing.

Dancing with a partner on the same uneven, unpredictable floor of grief is sometimes more challenging than dancing alone. It's a lot like the funhouse at the county fair, where the floor moves up, down, and sideways, all the while you are clinging to the ropes on the side that also move. It's quite hard to remain upright and maintain balance with all of the moving parts.

While it may sound like Clay and I were on the same page about how we processed this arduous journey, most of the time we weren't even in the same chapter. The good news is that we were at least in the same book, with the same goals for how we wanted our story to end. Like other steps of our journey, this one would also take much patience and persistence if we were to be victorious on our renewed quest for excellent health.

27

THE DOG DAYS OF SUMMER

Somehow after Andy's move, we muddled through the first six months of holidays, birthdays, and other significant events. Occasions that used to be so celebratory had now become excruciatingly painful. In addition, they now seemed to be constant and looming around every corner.

Valentine's Day starts the year off, followed pretty quickly by Easter, Andy's birthday, Mother's Day, our anniversary, Father's Day, Clay's birthday, and finally ending June with my birthday. None of these occasions ever bothered me in the least before Andy moved, but now all they seemed to do was emphasize that someone special was missing. There was an empty chair at all our gatherings, and the uncomfortable silence around our so-obviously missing person was deafening.

All these days seemed larger than life and needed to be anticipated and managed so they didn't end up managing us. I didn't dare ever let any one of these tough occasions sneak up on me or else my emotions would get the best of me pretty quickly.

I learned a couple of things early on. Having a plan to maneuver through these events was extremely helpful. Staying busy with family and friends made the time pass a little more easily. Also, understanding that almost like magic, 'the day after' always brought with it a sense of relief. I was sure that if I could get through each designated day, I would feel better, and that the weight of the world would be off my shoulders—at least temporarily—by the very next morning.

For Clay and me, this would be the first summer in thirty-two years with no kid activities. Since the early days of our marriage, our lives had been orchestrated around our four wonderful children and their various pursuits. This was certainly going to require an abrupt shift in our mental processes. Every day of the week, since I could remember, had had to be thought out way in advance and we nearly always followed our schedule to a tee. Now, what were we to do with ourselves?

Because of Andy's passing, our other kids, grandkids and friends were suddenly thrown into the spotlight. Looking back, I feel so fortunate that we were surrounded by so many people who were eager to fill the void that once was occupied by Andy.

As soon as the rest of Andy's junior year was over, we began planning our first charity baseball tournament to be held at the beginning of November 2013. Gathering volunteers and forming our board of directors quickly became a welcome diversion from the grief.

While this was happening, and seemingly out of the blue, a group of Andy's friends and their parents began planning a tree-planting ceremony at the school, down by the baseball field. Fortunately, I was on a first-name basis with the principal, so I knew we had more than a fair chance of pulling this off. Being sensitive to the mental well-being of the entire student body was always a priority for me and our foundation, and we'd hoped to hold the ceremony while school would be out, so as to avoid creating too much emotional upheaval for all the kids.

With the approval of the school administration, the precise spot and date for the tree planting was determined. With the addition of a rather large boulder that would bear a beautiful plaque engraved with a dedication to Andy, this dedication would also serve as the perfect memorial for this young man who so adored baseball and his high school teammates. The boulder would sit right in front of the tree for everyone to feast their eyes on and enjoy as they approached the bleachers. Plus, the tree would provide some much-needed additional respite from the oftentimes brutal Arizona sun.

Word about our upcoming tree-planting ceremony had spread by way of email, social media, and good old-fashioned word-of-mouth. Degan's parents, Jim and Cindy Harte, had picked out and delivered the boulder to its proper location. Blaze's parents, Scott and Danielle Bohall, had designed and arranged for the memorial plaque, which had been securely mounted to the boulder a day or so prior.

At the appointed date and time, countless parents, coaches, teachers, and friends arrived with shovels and lots of boxes of Kleenex. And last but certainly not least, the large Arizona desert tree had been delivered to the predetermined site beside the bleachers. It was the perfect spot for Andy's tree, and everyone who saw it said so. There wasn't another place that my Andy would rather be than at the very field where he had spent so many unforgettable days and nights.

Having visited Andy's memorial tree many times since that special day, I've watched it grow into a popular place for people to gather and seek shelter from the hot sun. Throughout the years, I have seen kids hang little notes and balloons on the branches in honor and memory of Andy. They are each such thoughtful and loving tributes—my throat tightens with emotion whenever I see them hanging there, for all the world to bear witness.

A couple years after Andy's friends had graduated, a new principal was hired for the high school. I could see the writing on the wall about the memorial and I did not want to wait for the phone call. So, I notified the principal that we'd be relocating the boulder to my daughter Beth's house for safekeeping. He thanked me, and that was that.

Just like that, the chapter on Andy's junior year was closed.

28

COUNTING THE DAYS

I held my breath when senior year at Andy's former high school was about to begin. I kept reliving, in my mind and heart, all the plans and dreams we'd had for this amazing kid. Remembering all too well each of our other children's senior years only added to my angst. Besides the memories, it was impossible to avoid all the social media hype for each of Andy's friends as they reached the various milestones, unless I just turned off the entire outside world.

Down deep I knew that facing my new reality head-on was what would ultimately serve me and my family best. That didn't mean that I had to participate in everything all the time; rather, I could attend only the little bits and pieces here and there that my still-bruised heart was ready to handle. I reminded myself fairly frequently that every phone call I made or received, or comment I read from others on social media, was strengthening my resolve to survive and gave me confidence that I could go on.

In addition to the inevitable arrival of normal, everyday occurrences, as the eleventh of each month approached, my stomach would start to ache, and my heart would quietly cry out in anguish. Not only was I counting the days since Andy had moved to Heaven, I was also counting the months until the one-year anniversary would arrive. With each passing day and week, we were becoming a tiny bit stronger and were able to breathe a little easier, but as December 11th grew closer, it felt as if we were sliding back to ground zero. We were losing our footing and our emotional control was headed straight out the door.

There were moments when I felt as if I could step out of my body and mind and watch all that was going on around and inside me as a third-party observer. It was during those times that I realized how important it would be for me to stay busy and make plans for every waking moment that I possibly could. I am thankful for this insight as it contributed greatly to my well-being.

While I instinctively knew what to do for myself, this was not always helpful for everyone else in the family. Learning to let them process their grief was hard, but I knew that it was necessary, in the long run, for their own mental health.

This was a challenge for me because, first and foremost, I am a natural fixer. I wanted so badly to help them all feel better. Secondly, after you lose one child, there is usually a fair degree of panic for the health and safety of your other children that creeps right into your subliminal consciousness, whether or not you want it to. I tried to be calm, but it was clear this was going to take some serious retraining of my thoughts and mind.

Part of this first year was spent traveling to North Dakota to spend time with Josh, who was still stationed at Minot Air Force Base. Since Andy's passing, Clay and I had flown up to see him and Kristin in January, July, and now September. This was not only part of my own therapy of keeping busy, but also our conscious effort to make sure that our other children knew how much we loved and needed them, too.

I have watched so many other grieving parents stay lost in their pain, sometimes for several years after their children's transitions. Sadly, perhaps without them even realizing it, this is often detrimental to their living children. Ever since that fateful day, I made sure to attend any and every function humanly possible in which any of my kids and grandkids were participating. I was grateful for all the opportunities because I needed them as gentle reminders for my tender heart that life does, indeed, go on.

Regardless of all that time spent with Josh, sadly for us, his pain would eventually lead him to cut off all ties with his wife and all of our family. To this day, we have no communication with this cherished son of ours. We continue to pray for our Josh each day and ask God to help him find his way back to us whenever the time is right.

During that first year, Michael was still stationed overseas, so being together with him was not possible. We tried as best we could to stay in contact with him via snail mail letters and Skype, but this distance of time and space would prove to be disastrous for Michael and his life as it existed prior to Andy's passing.

I could probably write an entire book on Michael's journey of physical and emotional devastation caused by an inability to process his pain within military confines. A couple years after Andy's move, Michael came back to Arizona following his honorable discharge. Though he'd successfully completed his military service, Michael would eventually come to lose his house, his wife, and on three occasions nearly his life. While Michael's situation is still far from perfect, he is slowly rebuilding his life.

Our daughter Beth, on the other hand, seemed to be weathering this storm much like I was. She not only had three young children to focus on, but her nursing background gave her an extra dose of resilience. Beth and I would come to lean on each other more than we did anyone else. We'd readily switch roles back and forth of being mother and daughter to one another.

Beth's children and her career kept her hopping, and she seemed as dependent on having a busy schedule as I was. As I've said, planning one's path of grieving and coping is critical for a faster healing process to take hold. I learned to be in charge, rather than allow my grief process to rule me. Beth continues to be a tremendous source of comfort and joy for me, even to this day.

In the back of all our minds, the inevitable one-year anniversary date was looming large on the horizon. Each and every one of us was dreading it. Already by September, the countdown had officially begun, and we knew we needed a plan of action if we were to survive.

It seemed deliberate that we were all doing activities that would lead us up to that day. Josh had begun training as a triathlete, Michael was planning a flag raising ceremony in Andy's honor while on his boat in the Persian Gulf, and Beth, Clay and I were busy planning a baseball tournament in remembrance of Andy. But nothing specifically was planned yet for that pivotal day.

Before it arrived, we still had a few months to get through, as well as the start of the grueling holiday season.

29

TELETUBBIES

Every parent remembers certain television shows or movies that we identify with our children specifically—typically something our children would watch over and over again, which left an indelible imprint in our brains. Over the years, there were times I thought I could repeat an entire movie verbatim because I had watched it so many times with one of my kids. Or maybe it was a song that played constantly on the radio or on their boombox when they were little.

Whatever it is, this memory will take us instantly back to the time and period that represents a certain stage of our children's lives. The images are so vivid that we might find ourselves getting goosebumps and smiling broadly, without even the least bit of effort. Like being transported by a time machine backward to a very special time with our children.

While this might make some parents sad, I have quite a different reaction. I am always so thankful for those memories when they come, and for the time Clay and I got to spend with all our kids. I choose to smile and remember—but not all of my family responds in the same way I do. Everybody copes differently and I try my best to allow each of them to have their own processes.

One such memory for Andy and me was the pre-school television show, Teletubbies. No, it wasn't Mr. Rogers or Sesame Street. Rather, it was a funky little cartoon show on the BBC. I'm not even sure how we discovered it, but Andy was instantly hooked. With such characters as Tinky-Winky, Dipsy, Laa and Po, who could blame him? What I remember most is that it was a happy show and the characters were just so darn cute. These four delightful characters had televisions implanted on the front surfaces of their bellies that showed real children having fun playing. For some reason, this odd little show mesmerized Andy, so much so that we would sometimes use it as a soothing tool to help him fall asleep.

The summer that Andy was two, Clay and I took all four kids to San Diego for a week. We had rented a house on the beach so it would be easy for us to haul all of the beach equipment directly from the patio down to the water. This was to be one of our craziest but most memorable trips ever. To accommodate all the kids and fun paraphernalia, we would need to take an SUV and a truck, which we fortunately had.

Each of our kids, including Andy, was permitted to bring a friend—but Beth managed to talk us into allowing her to bring both of her best friends. This meant that we had nine kids with us on this trip, ranging in age from eighteen to two. Talk about having lost our minds. We definitely had by the end of the week, but wow, what a great time was had by all.

Massive amounts of towels and wet bathing suits were draped across the backs of nearly every chair and hung on hooks on the walls and doors all over the house. Sandcastle building shovels, rollerblades, umbrellas, beach chairs, boogie boards, frisbees, sunscreen, snacks, drinks… on and on went the list of gear needed each day for our fun adventure.

Making sure that everyone was slathered in sunscreen and hydrated was a full-time job. Meal planning was another enormous undertaking. But thankfully, Clay loved preparing and cooking the meals, so I frolicked around the beach and ocean with all the kids. I loved riding the waves most of all, and the kids got such a kick out of doing it with me.

Life was so simple then. In a heartbeat, I'm sure we'd all wish to go back to that time and space if we could. It seemed as if everything was in perfect Divine order, and as it should be.

Earlier, as we were packing to head over to San Diego (about a five-hour drive from Phoenix) for our amazing vacation, I realized we were missing a couple essentials—our television and video cassette recorder. Since our rented beach home did not come equipped with a television, we had to be certain we'd have a way to keep our active toddler Andy entertained. With all of the possible levels of commotion from our eighteen-, sixteen-, and thirteen-year-old kids and their friends, we weren't about to chance any unnecessary outbursts from our two-year-old. In anticipation, we spent several days recording hour after hour of episodes from his beloved Teletubbies. Relieved that I thought of this before it was too late, we packed up our TV with our VCR and headed out on the road to California.

One of our last days spent at the beach house was really something quite special. By the end of a long week in the sun, sand, and water, nearly everyone was worn out and had had enough sunshine for a while. Late that afternoon, as Clay and I made our way back to the house from the beach, we happened upon the most precious sight. All the kids and their friends, spread out on the floor and nearby couches, were snuggled around Andy, watching and singing the Teletubbies songs right along with him.

These are the kinds of memories we love holding tight within our minds and hearts. While I sometimes still wish we could go back, I am forever thankful that all our children and their best friends were together with Clay and I that wonderful summer.

30

AND THEN THE RAINS CAME

The fields were reserved and the teams were all signed up for what was to be a fabulous first Andy Hull Memorial Baseball Tournament. All the hard work of our volunteers and time spent in our many planning meetings had paid off. This two-day event would be played at the baseball fields of three neighboring high schools: Sandra Day O'Connor, Mountain Ridge, and Boulder Creek.

All had agreed to loan us their fields, with some restrictions. In order to protect the grounds, we had to purchase liability insurance, as well as sign contracts with the district that all three of these schools were in. This was an arduous task, but we finally managed to pay the fees and get through all the red tape in time to pull off this exciting tournament.

We had reached out to all the various club teams and their coaches to ask for their participation, assuring them that the money we raised in fees would be used for scholarships at all three high schools, as well as equipment for their individual teams.

Not only would we be raising a significant amount of money, we would also be using this event as a suicide awareness and prevention function. Flyers and pamphlets had been gathered and mental health professionals had committed their time to assist at the games to answer anyone's questions about mental health. I wanted Andy's suicide to have a lasting and meaningful impact for as many people as we could possibly reach. After all, if this could happen to our Sunshine Andy, it could happen to anyone.

As the tournament week approached, excitement was building. Lots of intricate planning had gone into the execution of this tournament. How the teams progressed after a win or a loss was something that we left for the professionals to work out among themselves. I had asked two very special people—who happened to be two of Andy's favorite baseball coaches—to organize and run the teams and their correlating schedules. Jim Harte and Artie Cox had loved and mentored Andy from the moment they began coaching him, so they were delighted to come on board in this capacity.

During the very last summer before Andy moved to Heaven, he had been playing in a tournament in San Diego, where we had shared many great summers together as a family. One of the last games had been played on Coronado Island, where the field was nestled alongside picturesque San Diego Bay.

When Andy wasn't pitching, he was playing first base or right field, primarily because he was a lefty. He was always begging his coaches to let him play shortstop, which usually caused them to burst out laughing. Lefties never play shortstop.

Toward the end of this game, Andy was out in right field. Our team had a sizable lead, so everyone was quite relaxed and probably pretty tired after a week-long tournament. As I was sitting in the bleachers watching the game drag on, the batter hit one out to Andy in right field. Andy seemed to be in a daze because that ball flew right over his head without his making so much as a single muscle movement. This was so unusual, as Andy had always been drawn to the ball like a magnet. Nothing ever got past him.

I remember Artie asking him, when they all came off the field, "What happened out there, son?" Andy just shrugged his shoulders, and with a sheepish grin said, "I guess I was just watching that boat go by out in the bay." Artie laughed and shook his head at my crazy kid.

Winning was important to Artie and Andy, but neither of them ever got too cranked up about it and for that I was also very appreciative because, Lord knows, there were some terrible, mean and abusive coaches throughout Andy's years in baseball. Jim and Artie were definitely two of the good guys.

About a week before the memorial tournament, I started getting weather alerts on my phone for the upcoming weekend. *Okay, so what's a little rain?* We had certainly played during many an inclement weather event, sitting under our umbrellas, warmed by propane heaters and massive amounts of blankets. One might think that we lived in Minnesota, but for Arizonans, forty degrees was a regular arctic blast, so we were always well-prepared for the cold.

The calls started coming in from worried coaches and organizers, most of whom I knew were quite used to playing through this type of weather. So, I began to get a little nervous. Nonetheless, I kept assuring all of them that this tournament was part of a higher plan for good and therefore would not be thwarted.

They weren't buying it.

In the midst of all this, Clay had been offered a fabulous position back up in North Dakota. This job had come out of the blue after a former co-worker had recommended him. We needed this job badly because we had been financially wiped out by Clay's cancer and the financial crash of 2008 and the years that followed.

Physically, Clay was ready to go back to work, and emotionally he really needed to. He was scheduled to start work on the Wednesday after the tournament, which would allow him to stay for at least one day of it. Clay would have to leave Phoenix on Sunday so that he would have enough time—approximately two days—to drive up to North Dakota and also find a place to live. This assignment looked like it would probably last eighteen months, so finding a suitable long-term place would be important and probably a little challenging, since the oil boom was in full swing and vacancies were quite difficult to snag.

While Clay was busy packing for this new adventure, I was practically watching the weather nonstop, which continued to worsen as the weekend approached. Believe it or not, Phoenix does get rain, but on average, we receive only seven inches per year. According to the latest forecast, we were about to be deluged with potentially half of our annual rainfall in just a couple of days, and right smack on top of our tournament. Still, I was holding my breath and crossing my fingers that this forecast was overblown. After all, many a weather forecast had been way off in the past, and I was praying for it to be totally wrong this time, too.

Early on the week of the tournament, teams began pulling out. By Thursday, I could see the writing on the wall, as the weather radar did indeed show a massive storm headed right for typically sunny Phoenix, Arizona. On Friday morning, when I realized that our fate had been delivered to us by this untimely fluke of a storm, I cancelled the event. With a heaviness in my chest and tears streaming down my face, I realized, once again, that the twists and turns of life were not matching up with my well-intentioned expectations or plans.

I began making the calls and arranging for the return of the funds that had been paid by the various teams. Some of them kindly told me to keep the money in honor of Andy and to use it for our newly formed Andy Hull's Sunshine Foundation. These generous donations gave us an early financial boost for the work that we had already begun with the distribution of scholarships. With this infusion of money, we could begin building for the upcoming years.

In addition to all the plans we'd made, we had also purchased thousands of gorgeous bright yellow smiley-face T-shirts—as part of the 'face' of our foundation to the world. I knew they would come in handy for our many future activities, but for now they had to be stored away, along with lots of other fantastic plans for this cancelled tournament.

With a suddenly wide-open schedule, I decided to hitch a ride with my hard-working husband to North Dakota and help get him get situated. With a warm hug and a couple of tears, Clay shared his enthusiasm for having my company, even though he, too, was disappointed about the turn of events. He hadn't relished driving up there alone, but he was more than willing to take on this challenge for the sake of his mental and physical health, as well as our financial well-being.

One of us was going to have to go to work and I couldn't be more thankful to him for assuming this responsibility. I was quite content and busy with the day-to-day operations of starting a new non-profit organization. There was always so much to do, which not only filled my time, but also provided me with a renewed sense of purpose.

The rain did indeed fall as predicted. In fact, it poured buckets. Our lovely desert state was drowned by record amounts of gushing water. Dry riverbeds were suddenly running to the brim, streets were flooded, and the baseball fields were totally soaked. Sad as it was, it would have been impossible for us to continue with our plans for a winter baseball event, even if we had tried.

When it's raining in the Arizona desert, it's a sure bet that it's snowing in the mountains. This would no doubt impact our drive north. This drive—while somewhat precarious—forced us to slow down and savor the precious time that Clay and I had with each other. We allowed ourselves to unwind and relax a bit as we made our way through the freshly blanketed winter wonderland.

Up we went through the Rockies, and it could not have been any more beautiful. We stopped to snap pictures of antelope, deer, buffalo, and a few soaring eagles that seemed to be guiding our journey. Clay is like most men when they get focused on the task at hand, and he was really getting into this drive. Every time I saw something precious, I'd yell, "Stop, look at that!" He would groan and then kindly acquiesce to my request for yet another picture.

This trip took longer than originally planned, due to the inclement weather and my endless pleadings for pictures, but we finally arrived safe and sound on the evening before Clay was due to begin working. Since I was there with him this time, I could spend my days finding a nice place for him to live and Clay could head on into work.

Upon our arrival in Dickinson, North Dakota, we first checked into a hotel. Then off to our newly assigned jobs we went. Clay's days were unbelievably long, with twelve-hour shifts and a thirteen-days-on-and-one-off schedule, but the paychecks more than made up for this. This assignment turned out to be way more lucrative than anything we had ever done in our lives and would end up saving us financially.

I was reminded of the many blessings of closed doors and also the gift of rain.

31

ALMOST THERE

Clay and I spent our first Thanksgiving without Andy in an apartment in North Dakota, surrounded by many other workers in the oil field who were also without their loved ones. With the exodus of many of our family and friends after Andy's move, it had become obvious that we would have to learn to create family for ourselves wherever we went. Sometimes that sense of belonging would only be for a season, but no matter how long they were with us, our work family filled the void that was left by our physical distance from the rest of our biological family.

For the first couple of years after Andy moved to Heaven, Josh and his wife, Kristin, were still a major part of our lives and, as luck would have it, they were still living in North Dakota. For our first Thanksgiving away from home, Josh had thoughtfully offered to bring his fryer and a turkey to our apartment, so we could all share this holiday together. We happily accepted and invited a number of other people to join us.

Even though we were all in the same state, the military base where Josh was stationed was about three hours from us, so this was quite a feat to pull off, especially in the dead of winter. With all of the ice and blowing snow, the roads in North Dakota were quite treacherous during the winter months. New meaning was attached to the word "winter," as I had never before experienced anything like this kind of cold.

I was surprised that this didn't seem to faze the locals. Life went on even while it was snowing and below zero. Back home, we were used to staying indoors whenever the thermostat dropped below forty degrees. We would put on our turtlenecks and warm socks and light a fire in the fireplace. It certainly was not advisable to go outside in that kind of "harsh" Arizona environment.

Before that first winter in North Dakota, we hadn't known how much energy and preparation it would take to live and work in that frigid environment. I had done my best to set up Clay's home away from home so that he could be as comfortable as possible.

Now, after surviving three brutal winters in various cities in North Dakota, I look back and laugh at that mindset.

One such winter we had a wind chill factor of minus 65 degrees. I didn't know one could survive those kinds of temperatures, let alone work in them. Yet, off to work Clay went. People were out and about, going on with their lives, headed to the grocery stores and Walmart. Even the children went off to school, bundled up like walking mummies, but nonetheless off they trudged through the snow. Nothing seemed to stop these determined, hearty people of the north.

I began the usual preparations for a Thanksgiving dinner, baking pies and creating all of the other wonderful side dishes that had become staples in our annual holiday feasts. Maintaining some semblance of normalcy was especially important to me. Even though our world had been turned upside-down, this didn't mean everything we had enjoyed in the past should suddenly become invalid.

In fact, I really craved those traditions, as I hoped they might provide some comfort and be the glue that would hold us together. Remembering all the times I had baked with my mom and/or my grandmother helped me understand that I could also hold onto the memories and traditions that I had shared with Andy. I realized that I could do this for the rest of my life.

Interestingly, this also would be my first Thanksgiving in a number of decades without my mom, since she was back in Arizona and I was in North Dakota. We were all in uncharted territory that was new and uncomfortable, and I feared that blazing new trails would prove to be an everyday occurrence.

Given our current state of grief and remote location, Thanksgiving was as much a success as it possibly could have been. It helped tremendously to have Josh and Kristin with us, as well as several other workers from Clay's job.

Every holiday that we survived was providing us with a new, strong foundation of confidence that we would survive. Yes, it was tough, but we hit it head-on and learned the tricks of managing our ever-changing emotions. To be clear, though, "managing" doesn't mean that there weren't still many days filled with tears, or that the all-too-familiar gut ache of loss had disappeared. It did mean that we could choose where and when those moments were acceptable for the people in our presence and in our current surroundings. We were going to be the masters of this journey—one day, one minute, one second at a time.

Clay spent most of his days at work, and when he was home, he was thoroughly exhausted. Not only did the work tire him out, but having to fight the bitter cold every day was wearing. Because this left me alone without any real distractions or company, I decided, shortly after our Thanksgiving gathering, to return to our home in Phoenix.

As Clay and I reflect back on this time, we both clearly see how his work in North Dakota provided a respite from most of his emotional pain. He was either so busy or so exhausted that there was almost no time or energy left to reminisce or long for his beloved Andy. For Clay, this allowed his brain to begin to heal and provided some much-needed time to soften the blow of his immense loss.

Both of our circumstances were just what the doctor had ordered for our optimum healing. We were blessed with the uncommon ability to allow each other to grow through the pain at our own pace and by our own processes. Neither of us felt threatened or infringed upon by the other's way of coping. We learned quickly that patience, gentleness, and kindness were the essential tools needed if we were to survive and move forward with our marriage and lives.

We were almost there. One more week and that dreaded, difficult day would be upon us. As it happens, it would be a defining moment for many days, months, and years to come.

32

ONE YEAR

How did we get here? How did life go on after such a horribly dark day in our lives? How in the world did we survive that awful first year? This day had been lurking around the corner since the very day Andy left us. We could not begin to see, at that time, how we could navigate these unknown waters without drowning. The blinders on our minds' eyes were providing us with shelter from our dreaded journey.

If we had tried to look at the year ahead and analyze it or project what those months would look like, it would have been incomprehensible and way too painful. Living our lives in tiny bites of existence had become our salvation. We didn't look too far in advance, nor did we spend too much time gazing into the rearview mirror. Most of the time, being awake and aware in the present moment helped us focus on our daily blessings.

Like the light that Andy had been to everyone throughout his life, it occurred to me that we needed to honor our precious boy by sending light and love up to him in Heaven. That light needed to be bright enough so that Andy would be sure to see it from Heaven, and we'd have to do this in a venue that would hold all his friends and family who wanted to share in this auspicious moment.

Because it would be in the middle of winter in Arizona, we knew we'd need a roaring bonfire and lots of hot chocolate. From there, the vision for what to do came to me clear as day. Andy's name would be spelled out with lots and lots of pre-arranged candles, spread widely across our Arizona desert landscape at night, for all to see.

For the previous month or so, Andy's friends had been messaging me with their inquiries about the happenings of "the day." From all accounts, it looked like there were more than one hundred kids who wanted to attend whatever event we would plan. Plus, I was certain that some of their parents, whom I knew, would want to be there with us, too. And most of my family would also be there to support us at this big event. Michael appeared to be the only one of our family who would be unable to come home for this big affair, since he was still stationed out in the Persian Gulf. Clay, Josh, and Kristin were all planning on coming home from North Dakota, so it looked like we would have a full house.

As plans began to take shape, it became clear to me that our home would be the perfect—and only—place to hold such a gathering. We had a ginormous house with lots of indoor and outdoor living space, as well as an acre and a quarter of beautiful desert back yard. Parking could prove to be challenging, but we could easily shuttle people back and forth from a neighboring street, if need be. To top it off, I knew just the right spot to lay out my inspired multi-candle Andy memorial.

When our home was newly built, Clay was ranked fifth in the world for his age bracket in the weight pentathlon. And what does every track star need in his own back yard? An area for practicing his shot-put, discus, and hammer throws.

Accordingly, a large, flat, smooth spot in our beautiful landscape had been laid out and designated Clay's very own throwing area. As much as he supported Andy's athletic endeavors, Andy likewise supported Clay in his, so I could not think of a more perfect spot for the location of my special Andy candle tribute.

After the disastrous weather front had derailed our baseball tournament, I was a little gun-shy about planning another big outdoor event. But I was still a steadfast believer in all things being possible, so plan ahead we did.

Step one was purchasing all the necessary snacks and drinks for lots of hungry and thirsty teenagers. Gathering wood for the big bonfire was next, as well as obtaining additional firewood for our various fireplaces that were scattered around our property. We would also need some large heaters for the outdoor patios where people could sit and visit. We picked up plates, cups, napkins and eating utensils, and borrowed chairs from some of our wonderful friends and neighbors. Then we were tasked with locating several boxes of tiny white candles for setting up my desert design.

Planning just the right entertainment for the evening was to be the final detail left to check off my list. I had met a guy named David Sheehee a few months earlier, who sang in some local venues and had a fabulous voice. We had become somewhat personally acquainted with one another, so I was hopeful that he might donate an appearance at our big event.

David was a one-man show, a singer-songwriter who also played acoustic guitar and happened to be quite entertaining. When I received his acceptance of my proposal, I was thrilled because that had been the final piece left for our celebration, and everything was falling into place. Even the weather seemed to be blessing us by shaping up in our favor.

Finally, "the day" arrived. In some ways, it was like reliving our son's poignant memorial service. The adrenalin that was flowing through all of us would carry us well into the night. I also suspect that some degree of shock was still occupying our brains and sheltering us from the full reality and gravity of the day.

Just in case the weather would suddenly take an unexpected unfavorable turn, I waited until the very last moment to lay the candles out on the lawn. It turned out to be a beautiful, cloudless night with billions of stars clearly visible, and I was thrilled.

The fires were a welcoming place for us all to hang out together and reminisce about Andy. Everybody had a story to share about their cherished best friend. It reminded me of how amazed I was that Andy seemed to have been "best friend" to each of these amazing kids. I loved listening to each of them tell their stories, and I hoped and prayed they would never forget this precious boy whom I loved so dearly.

Those who had been helping me plan this party joined me in handing out dozens of lighters so that when the appointed time came, they could all help light up this brilliant tribute to our Sunshine. The night wore on, and finally the time had come to signal an ending—as well as a new beginning. Just as the last of the candles were lit, two of Andy's favorite songs by Florida Georgia Line, "Cruise" and "Get Your Shine On," were playing from a speaker that I had attached to my phone, and we all stood somberly remembering, with great fondness, a life that was gone from us way too soon.

Even Andy showed up for his own memorial event. Take a look at the picture in the center of this book of our incandescent display and you'll see Andy's blue spirit hovering over us against the backdrop of the night sky—right beside all the glorious, luminous candles.

Year one was now down in the history books, and our future was staring right at us. For this brief moment, though, I would appreciate the rest and reprieve that always soothed me on the mornings after. I had come to count on this relief, and while the tears would always still flow, they would gently caress my cheeks and bring me great comfort as they rolled.

GARRETT MARTIN SAVOIE
8\30\1991 — 11\17\2010
FUN LOVING, ADVENTUROUS, KIND, SON, BROTHER— LOVED!!

33

NEW YEAR

Unlike everyone else, our "New Year" began on December 12, rather than on the first of January. From the moment Andy moved to Heaven, our family's calendar had been permanently altered and redefined in perpetuity.

Each year, on the morning after Andy's day occurred, we'd begin counting the weeks and months for the next year. Funny, it no longer seemed to matter how old we were on our birthdays, or even how old Andy would have been on his. All that mattered was how long it had been since our beloved Andy had left us.

For the first couple of years, time stood still, seemingly frozen by this unforeseen tragedy. While we could surely see the days and months changing on the calendar, it felt like we were spending much of each day stuck in quicksand. We felt like heavy bodies with empty minds—and when the cloud of emptiness subsided, swirling waves of sadness and pain occupied the space. Neither place was one that I could bear to stay in for very long. It was such a strange existence; almost like being caught in a whirlpool that was holding me captive until I could finally find my way out.

Thankfully, while in the process of reading eighty books during that first year, I had thoroughly investigated and implemented several alternative methods of coping. Did the books fix me or make me feel better while I was reading them? Generally speaking, I would say no. But what they did was help me form a new foundation upon which my life without Andy could be built. Unaware of this at the time, I was essentially rewiring my thought processes with healthier ways of thinking and coping with life.

In reality, it wasn't until a few years later that I would come to recognize the full impact of everything I had done during that first very difficult year. In some ways, it was like being given a clean slate to work with, as many of the reference points for my life had been wiped away. Things that I had thought were true or important no longer held the same value or meaning for me.

Everything was colored by this new twist of fate in my life. Well, not exactly colored to begin with—as everything around me felt so black. But in relatively short order, I learned to add color back into the pages of my existence, even if a little slowly at first. If I had waited for outside circumstances to impact my life, the ink on the pages would have remained black for much longer—and, possibly, forever. Drastic times required drastic measures.

Attending the Helping Parents Heal meetings, reading empowering books, forming Andy Hull's Sunshine Foundation, listening to music that I find uplifting, exercising, meditating, et cetera, were all tools I used from the moment Andy left. I needed every one of them to survive.

By the end of the first year, the use of these tools had begun to make a significant change in who I was and how I would live my life. Repetitive retraining of my thoughts and actions to positive and healthy pathways would eventually become a natural way of living for me. Just like with an athlete who trains and trains, eventually the mind and body become accustomed to these great habits one is developing.

Having patience and persistence throughout this process is equally as important as retraining the mind. While it's easy to feel discouraged in the very beginning, we all must keep pushing through. Like going to the gym. The first few visits are miserable, and the results are never noticed immediately. In order for anything to have enough value, you have to set tangible goals and work past the pain.

The same is true for loss of any kind. What is it that you want your life to look like from here forward? Defining and setting a clear image in your head of what this would look like for you is critical. This is known as mental imaging—or visualization—of what you want. This is not a passive process, however, and if you want to move forward, you must decide every day that this is what you want for your life. You must first determine the goal, then make a list of strategies or ways that you can accomplish your whole endeavor, and then practice, practice, practice.

This is exactly what I had been doing during that challenging first year, and now the fruits of my labor were finally beginning to pay off. Not overnight, of course, but little by little the light was starting to shine again on my life, and the colors were starting to brighten.

Sometimes, I would feel inclined to take a break from this mental workout, but now more than ever it was critical for me to continue to build and solidify what I'd started. The energy that it took to sustain this is why many people give up at various stages along the way.

First of all, we in the twenty-first century have been programmed for instant gratification. If what we want doesn't happen right away, we too often throw in the towel. Many times, it's too soon. Most things that are worthwhile in life require a great deal of effort and attention to obtain them, and this is certainly no different.

Giving myself permission to sit in whatever space I was in allowed me to gather the courage and strength necessary to forge onward. Sometimes that was a day, or a week, but usually not too long because that might have reversed all the headway that I had already made. A stagnant mind is no healthier than a stagnant pool of water. In order for it to be safe, it has to be fed and renewed on a regular basis.

As the days and weeks of our "new year" moved on, I continued to reinforce all the newly formed mental and physical habits I had developed. Christmas of 2013 came and went, as well as the traditional New Year. New routines had been formed; life was moving forward, and so were we.

Beth was starting her new nursing career and the grandkids were growing and thriving. A few months after Andy moved, she had graduated from nursing school. What an amazing accomplishment this was, especially considering her state of shock and trauma, and all the responsibilities she had taken on as a result of our family's loss. I couldn't have been more proud of my brilliant daughter for the numerous ways in which she was showing her kids how to survive a traumatic event. As a result, Beth's children were responding with the same kind of resiliency that she was—and that greatly relieved me.

Michael came home that spring and began a long and ugly journey forward. When he was still overseas, our national news did a story on Michael paying tribute to his younger brother and also giving thanks to his wife for all her support. This proved to be only the start of his healing process. Unfortunately, Michael hadn't been able to do anything that even remotely resembled healing while he was living abroad, so his healing path was at ground zero, so to speak, when he first returned home.

Josh began seriously training to become an Ironman, which he would amazingly accomplish just one short year later. The term "Ironman" refers to a very strong man with remarkable endurance, and that was certainly Josh.

Still stationed in North Dakota when he began training, this process was very grueling due to that state's many months of inclement weather. In addition, his day job of being in charge of the Base Honor Guard kept Josh tremendously busy. The local press and news stations in Minot soon got wind of Josh's efforts toward winning triathlons and other such competitions, and began running articles and newscasts about his plans to become an Ironman in honor of his brother Andy.

Flying was becoming a monthly occurrence for me as I traveled to North Dakota to see both Josh in Minot, and Clay, who was still busily working in Dickinson. These trips always provided me with a welcome break from my everyday life without Andy, and they also gave my heart and brain some greatly needed reprieve.

I have often said that, for me, the second year was much tougher because the shock had worn off and reality had truly set in—all the more reason to have laid a reliable foundation of coping skills during that first year. Since so much of the outside support from others had dwindled or disappeared altogether, I would definitely need them.

The real work was now up to me.

34

SUDDENLY AN EXPERT

Andy Hull's Sunshine Foundation was now quite active in the local community and beginning to move into the international corners of the world. Since delivering my first presentation four months after Andy moved, word got out, and more and more schools began calling me to come and share our "You Matter!" message at their school assemblies.

As part of every talk I gave, we handed out hundreds of our "You Matter!" yellow wristbands for free. We encouraged every teacher, student, and school employee in attendance to take one for themselves and an extra one for someone they loved, to show them they mattered. We wanted to not only impact the audience in attendance, but we were also dedicated to delivering an uplifting message in our local community.

From the very beginning, branding had happened quite naturally. Yellow was the perfect color choice from the start, since Andy's nickname was Sunshine, and thus an integral part of the name of our foundation. T-shirts were yellow. Wristbands were yellow. Website was yellow.

Even though it originated from a dark and heavy topic, our message was uplifting.

We never shied away from talking about the how or why of Andy's death—at least to the best of our ability—and we always ended our conversations by expressing the importance of each and every one of us to each other. Everyone has a distinct purpose here on this Earth, and we were driving that point home with one connection, one presentation, and one wristband at a time.

Besides the schools, we began to receive requests from military bases, churches, rotary clubs, and many other organizations, to come and share our message of love, loss, grief, and hope. I was the presenter at each of these venues, with lots of great support from our board members and volunteers.

The events were videotaped and placed on the popular social media sites. Not only did this bring growth to our local notoriety, but requests for our wristbands began funneling in from across the globe. Soon we were shipping hundreds of these bands to Australia, Scotland, Ireland, Nicaragua, and Canada, as well as many other places within the United States. We always deliver our wristbands free of charge, so our fund-raising efforts needed to be stepped up in order to cover the big expense of international and domestic postage.

How odd, I thought, that I would now be considered an expert on suicide. Certainly, I was not a great example of how to prevent it. I had learned to identify the signs that had been there during the few months before Andy left, but that had gone unnoticed. I knew these warning clues could absolutely be used now to save the lives of millions of other people, if I could just continue to find the fortitude to expose myself, be vulnerable, and share my kid's incredible story. Maybe I could spare another mom and dad this terrible heartache.

My message began evolving with every talk, growing each time that I shared this grueling tale of life, loss, and then hope. Crafting an informational, as well as hopeful, message—all in the framework of this heavy topic—presented its share of challenges.

In addition, if I wanted to be called back by a school or referred, each talk had to be carefully adjusted for age appropriateness. Besides the fact that I had lost my son to suicide, my professional background was by no means aligned with this new direction. The only thing that leant itself well to this path was my ability to be an effective speaker, which had become quite evident when I had run for Congress several years prior.

Almost immediately after Andy moved, I began reaching out to mental health professionals for their help and support at my various events. They were eager to assist me on this journey for a couple of reasons. First, because I didn't have academic credentials, they wanted to be on hand to lend their expertise in the event they found it necessary. Second—and much later on down the road—their help came because they had seen enough of my presentations to hear the integrity and helpfulness of my message, and they offered to be of assistance in any ways they could. This process of becoming qualified in their eyes took several years before they fully supported me in my endeavors. I'm happy to report that we eventually became great partners on this suicide awareness and prevention fronts.

My message was comprised of three segments. The first, and by far the most difficult for me to share, was Andy's story—who he was in this world and how he came to leave. While there were many parts that brought a smile to my face, this piece was tough to get through, as it also reminded me of the kid I was sorely missing.

The second part was all about the emotional triggers. What are some things that can cause any of us to harm ourselves, even if we've never before considered doing so? While suicide is by far the worst reaction to life's difficulties, cutting, eating disorders, excessive intake and abuse of drugs and alcohol, and unhealthy relationships are also potential responses to negative input we receive from our surroundings. Some of the catalysts for self-harm come from social media, unhealthy friends, the actual alcohol or drugs, bullying, or low self-esteem. And that's just to name a few.

The third part of my speech always ended with teaching the audience members how to develop healthy coping skills, the effectiveness of which I had first-hand knowledge. All of the tools that I've mentioned in previous chapters were lifesaving for me. Reading empowering books, meeting with encouraging friends, listening to pre-selected music, exercise and or meditation, et cetera, were all essential for my own well-being. One might even wish to seek out a counselor or therapist if these self-help methods don't seem to be enough.

Word eventually made its way to newscasters about my "expertise" on the subject of suicide, and suddenly, anytime another tragedy occurred, I was on their list to be interviewed. Happily, I agreed to do any and all interviews because this was a two-way street. In the process of sharing my past experiences, I also had the opportunity to put in a plug for the work that our foundation was doing, so this turned out to be a win-win for both parties.

In the ensuing years, I have become accustomed to being an "expert" on suicide for the experiences I have had and all the coping tools I have utilized. This title is a curious thing to come to terms with after having gone through something so sad and horrific. Certainly, it's not anything that anyone would, in their right mind, wish to be so proficient in. I suspect that for most of us who gain such a title, it either stems from one's own personal experience or it might just be a morbid interest in the difficult subject matter.

Does anyone wake up one day and decide he or she wants to pursue a career in suicide prevention? Maybe, but so far, I haven't found anyone like that. Whatever the reason, suicide statistics are staggering, and it will take all of our collective efforts to stop this terrible epidemic.

Somewhere over the Rainbow

Jacen Cain
9/15/00 - 1/14/15

35

Blessed

I have heard the term "new-normal" quite often from other parents who have "lost" a child, as well as in the many books on grief that I briefly glanced at. "New normal" is commonly used as the description of life after loss. That particular way of labeling our lives didn't sit well with me at the beginning, nor does it now.

First, one has to ask, "What's normal?" This thought-provoking question could be asked before or after a tragedy of any kind. I had never really seen my life as something that could be defined one way or another or fit into a tidy box. It was an ever-changing, flowing stream, filled with any number of twists and turns. There were moments of calm, as well as times of extreme turbulence. Sometimes the water was crystal clear, while at other times it was murky.

From my perspective, the only way most people decide whether their lives are normal or not is by comparing themselves to others. I have always rebelled against the norm and I've preached to my kids endlessly that if they're doing what everyone else is doing, they should probably rethink their actions. I have always believed that life should be about the uniqueness of each person's journey, and I'm pleased to say that, for the most part, mine has been.

"Compare and despair," as I like to think of it, is unfortunately how we so often get ourselves into trouble. By comparing our experiences with that of our neighbors or friends, we can either feel like we are blessed or cursed—usually one or the other. Judgment of any kind is always the death of gratitude or appreciation for what we have been gifted.

I remember a presentation I gave one year, during a Mother's Day church service, where I spoke about this very subject. "What is a blessing?" I asked. "Am I no longer blessed because my son tragically died by suicide? Isn't that what it leads us to believe, if we claim that God had blessed us when things were going well? Does that mean that God has withdrawn his blessings on me because my kid died?"

In my opinion, this would conjure up images of someone holier than thou up there, passing out blessings to those of us who are hoping and praying to receive them. In no uncertain terms do I think that God did this to Andy, or to me and my family. I strongly believe that I'm just as blessed as the next person, regardless of how my son died. To me, it's all in the perception and ownership of our lives, and I have a choice about how I perceive and/or label all that happens to me.

Do I wish that this hadn't happened? Of course! I would gladly give up any personal growth I've accumulated just to have Andy back in my life. I would give anything to turn back the hands of time and have my son with me again. I grieve, and have grieved, the loss of my boy just like any other parent grieves the loss of her or his child. Yet nothing I do to propel my life forward diminishes the immense love I have for Andy and the crater that was left in my heart when he moved to Heaven.

I have also had to reevaluate the real meaning of the term "lost." Is Andy lost? No. I wholeheartedly believe that he has simply moved to another dimension, and with practice, I can still have a relationship with him. Not in the physical sense, but rather one that is more spiritual in nature.

Using the word "lost" is such a normal way for us to describe the death of a child or loved one. Frankly, we speak so often in terms of loss in our culture that it is challenging for us to find any other way to express ourselves. Yet, I find this to be an unfair representation of what really happens to us in the spiritual realm.

I have found it particularly important to be extremely selective about my choice of words that I speak, as well as the thoughts I allow in my head. If I am constantly going around talking about what or who I have lost, or who is or is not blessed, this makes me feel out of control.

As long as we give our ability to manage our lives over to others, we will continue to feel helpless in our grief. In essence, we are then left in limbo, waiting for someone else to fix us. By taking ownership of not only our emotions but our choices of the words we use, we can then begin to take back control over what we perceive as negative or unhappy experiences.

Did this work right off the bat? No! I had to practice changing my vocabulary and being selective and quite deliberate with all my words, so they would reinforce a positive thought process rather than one that is only more negative.

Then there are the ways I choose to respond to the cliché things people say when they talk about death with the bereaved, like:

"How are you?"

"Are you better?"

"God doesn't give you more than you can handle."

"Time heals all wounds."

"Your son's in a better place."

These are just a few of the things said to me by well-intentioned people right after Andy moved. I tell myself that they don't know better and I try hard not to blame them, but that hasn't always been easy.

Honestly, there were times I was tempted to punch people when they said such hurtful things to me. In time, though, I have come to understand that they didn't mean anything harmful by their statements.

Fortunately, they probably haven't ever experienced anything nearly as devastating as the "loss" of a child; and secondly, we as a society have not been taught what to say or how to help someone who is grieving.

As a direct result of the work I was doing in the aftermath of Andy's move, I found myself growing in two areas I had not anticipated—patience and love. As I've grown, it has been much easier for me to guide others in the proper verbiage and meaningful responses to someone else's anguish and pain. I've found that a little training from someone like me can go a long way. When it comes right down to it, most of us really do want to know how we can best support people we care for when they are hurting. It's just that usually, without some instruction, we don't really quite know how.

As for the term "blessed," I prefer to leave that word out of my vocabulary altogether and simply say that "I am grateful for my life." Being thankful puts me in a totally different state of mind and gives everything in my life a different hue. It also puts me in the driver's seat, which is where I am always most comfortable anyway.

I view making a choice to be thankful or grateful as different from feeling or stating that I am blessed. One is an action we choose; the other is a seemingly random gift from up above. Don't get me wrong. I do believe in a Higher Power and am certain that prayer is helpful. If we believe that God is a loving Creator, then we must also believe that He loves us. After all, love is the real reason that we are here.

So, we are blessed, just by the very gift of life we've been given. It's up to us to choose a healthy response to all the adventures that we will surely encounter along our journeys.

Just to be clear, I am not saying that we have to be happy or joyful all the time. It would be foolish for me to think that could even be possible. Typically, we learn what real love and pleasure are through experiencing pain and sorrow. This is one of the few times that a comparison is actually helpful.

With great love comes the potential for great pain. The yin and yang of this principle is in the world if we simply open ourselves up for a total life experience immersion.

I have spent many a day and night sobbing my eyes out over Andy's not being here with me in the physical realm anymore. Sometimes I just want to hug him and smell his special boy scent. I miss seeing my beautiful son being carefree and living his life with gusto, as he so often did.

What do I focus on now? This became my new challenge. What have I had that I've lost, or what do I feel I am missing? This is truly the key to overall happiness in life. From time to time, I ask myself, am I thankful for the sixteen amazing years that we were able to share with Andy? Or am I living in the painful sorrow of all the times we missed out on that could have, and should have, been?

My choice is the only right choice for me. I choose to be grateful and hold my memories of sweet Andy dear and close to my heart.

Looking forward, I am now in the driver's seat of my life, in charge of my emotional destiny.

REECE
LOYAL!
AWESOME SWIMMER!
GREAT FRIEND
SUPER COOL!
DOB 12-04-99
LOVE THIS KID
ANGEL DATE 3-27-2017

36

MILESTONES

January of 2014 would have been Andy's senior year of baseball. Once again, the boys voted unanimously to dedicate this last season to their treasured friend. Without a second thought, I vowed to myself that I would attend every game that I possibly could and I'd support their baseball endeavors to the best of my ability.

As much as I was happy to do so, some days were harder than others to be there. It would take some doing because I had to prepare myself mentally and emotionally before and after each game for my roller coaster ride full of joy and sorrow. Though it was not readily visible, I would usually arrive with a heavy heart, but would soon find myself, as in the past, all caught up in the joy of this wonderful game that both Andy and I loved so much. Even when it looked like our team was headed for a loss, I still found immense pleasure in being fully immersed in the moment.

Without a doubt, we all learned so much during this last season of varsity baseball. It was undeniable—at least to me— how much having a purpose and passion played into the end results of an action or a particular public event. Because these boys had a clear picture in their minds of how they wanted this season to look, it played out almost perfectly. I say "almost" because the end was not exactly the desired result—although the process of getting there was absolutely perfect.

Our team would go nearly undefeated again for the entire season, which took them all the way to the Arizona State Championship Playoffs at a huge major league stadium. Working your way through the brackets to end up at the final state championship game was the dream of every coach and player—and that's precisely what these talented young ballplayers did.

Our team and their excited entourage—including me—arrived at the pro ball stadium with fingers crossed, having sent many a prayer up to God and to Andy in Heaven, asking for this last game to have the fairy tale ending we'd been dreaming of. Although I was happy for all these kids who had worked so hard to get there, at times I found myself scanning the dugout, searching for the arrival of my dear leftie onto the field. The devastation of realizing that this would never again be possible is, even still, sometimes a bit much to handle.

The moment of truth finally arrived. Though they'd all done a great job and played their hearts out, in the end this game fell just short of the desired outcome. Technically, they had lost the game and were not crowned as the state champions. But in a much more valuable and long-lasting way, they had all become champions—not just to me, but to everyone.

They had learned about love and deep loss, and that the two can often coexist side by side. Remaining friendly with all of them, and talking with them over the years, would prove gratifying for years to come, as I watched these amazing young men face all the many challenges that everyday life can sometimes bring with it.

Besides attending the numerous baseball games, there was much work to be done in order to make an impact on the horrible suicide statistics. In 2013, suicide was the tenth leading cause of death for all ages, and there were more than 41,000 deaths by suicide in the United States alone.

Because of my run for Congress a few years prior, coupled with my own personal experience, I had suddenly become an asset to the Arizona chapter of the American Foundation for Suicide Prevention (AFSP). This group had tried in previous years to get a legislative bill passed through our state Congress that would make suicide education mandatory in all schools, but the bill had not been passed.

Having made many great connections throughout Arizona during 2010, when I'd run for office, I now could make inroads for the promotion of AFSP's various bills—while at the same time being useful for their foundation. Reaching out to some of the senators and representatives was a natural fit for my tenacious personality, and I was happy to do it. I rarely take no for an answer, and I'm also not easily deterred. I had no idea how much this would come in handy during the days and months that were to come.

Getting a bill signed into law is no small feat. The key to the game proved to be scheduling meeting after meeting with as many men and women of Congress as humanly possible.

Presenting the statistics and the need for this kind of education, all packaged around my own personal story, would continue to reinforce my resolve and passion for the journey that I humbly found myself on. I felt strongly that if we could save just one child, then this would all have been worth the grueling process of retelling my sad but uplifting tale.

After all the meetings were finished, the board members and I began testifying in front of four different committees in the House and Senate. At each of these scheduled hearings, I would put my name on the list as a speaker. Sometimes waiting for hours for our assigned time, the group of us from Andy Hull's Sunshine Foundation would sit in silence with the pain of what we were about to share. This was pure agony for nearly all of us.

When the moment would finally arrive, after all our coping skills had been taxed to the max, I would stand up and share the "what if's." For example, what if I, or any of the many other people who had come into contact with my son, had been educated on the warning signs of suicide and how to prevent it? Would the outcome have been any different? Wouldn't you want that possibility for your child? I always asked them to personalize it and think about their own precious children or grandchildren. Let's all put a face on this terrible killer, not just a number.

After all was said and done, Congress was not yet ready to make this a mandatory education bill. It ended up as simply an option for teachers to get continuing education credits if they chose to take a class on this subject. The actual bill, Arizona HB 2605, would eventually be signed into law by Governor Jan Brewer during the summer of 2014, with a special signing ceremony in her office.

While it was not what we had all hoped for, it was certainly a step in the right direction—if only a baby one. It would eventually pave the way for another law, passed in 2019, that requires all educators to receive training on suicide prevention. Unfortunately, not until the lives of another thirty-eight students were lost to suicide in just a few short months, all within neighboring schools.

Only then, and with much media attention, did our state government hear the cries and pleadings of these poor grieving parents. It has always fascinated me that it wasn't the parents of living children fighting for this law, but rather those who had already suffered great loss. We were all working so hard, lobbying to save someone else's child, not our own.

While all the baseball games and committee hearings were going on, another milestone came and went without Andy. How much can one broken heart take? His eighteenth birthday would soon be upon us and if I were to survive, I knew that a plan needed to be put into action.

There were still lots of kids hanging out at our house every day, almost as if we were all sitting around, waiting for Andy to burst through the front door in excitement. I did enjoy having their company and felt so privileged to hear the many new stories about Andy that I had not heard before. It's important to note that time spent together with all these kids was not a sad or even a somber time. We were really just giving thanks for all the great times we had spent with this amazing kid.

One of Andy's all-time favorite restaurants had been Panda Express, so we decided to have his eighteenth birthday celebration there. It just so happened that one of the home games for the varsity baseball team landed on Andy's birthday. This would no doubt make for a perfect lead-in to our gathering afterward.

So many of the ball team's fans, students and parents alike, wore their yellow T-shirts to the game—so much so that the bleachers looked like a vast sea of yellow. One of the player's moms brought yellow cupcakes, which were so cute and absolutely delicious. Lots of kids showed up with great big yellow balloons which were inflated and tied to Andy's tree in commemoration of him.

Normally, this would have been a great celebration, but it was definitely colored with a tinge of sadness that we all tried to mask as best we could. Strangely enough, it had been eighteen years since Andy came into our lives and almost eighteen months now since he moved.

I wound up feeling very ill with the flu that day, but still managed somehow to make an appearance. I noticed that whenever there was something that affected me emotionally, I tended to come down with some kind of physical ailment. I came to realize through this process that the mind and body are very closely linked. This was my body's way of displaying how badly my heart was still hurting. With time, I would learn to manage this better and keep myself not only mentally well, but physically healthy, too.

Adorned with our bright yellow smiley-face T-shirts, we celebrated the life of our precious Andy. It was a bittersweet day; nonetheless it was important to all of us that we acknowledge these days with joy, as opposed to sadness. Ignoring birthdays and holidays was not going to change our reality, but we could surely choose how we lived each and every one of them.

And then, high school graduation was upon us. The closer we got to this important day, the more the ache in my stomach and tightness in my chest had been building. Thankfully, I had been practicing for graduation during the previous eighteen months, just as I had processed all of Andy's other missed milestones. By now, I was better prepared for the inevitable and had come up with a plan of action for all the days and weeks leading up to it.

Each time I went to the mailbox and received a graduation announcement for one of Andy's friends, I had to fight the pain and regret that I was feeling inside. After all the work I had done in the previous months, I did not want to sink into a pit of despair. I also did not want to be missing in action for all these kids who had meant so much to my son—and who had come to mean so much to me, too. These young men and women had become my treasured friends;

I needed them. I think it's more than fair to say that we all needed each other.

With a clear mental image of how I was going to handle the upcoming graduation, I set out on a mission. I may be a strong woman, but I felt that attending the graduation ceremonies and/or parties would be above and beyond the call of my duty—and frankly, a little more than I felt I could handle.

Acknowledging them, though, was totally different. I decided that each of Andy's close friends would be honored and celebrated for all their accomplishments with a special memento from me. Without exception, I knew exactly what I wanted to give to each of Andy's friends. Now I just needed to get with it and arrange for these precious items to be packaged in time to be hand-delivered by me to each of them before I made my exodus out of town.

As soon as this chapter of our lives would conclude, I had been planning to drive back up to North Dakota to spend the summer with Clay. This would be the ending of one season and the beginning of a brand-new chapter for all of us. Andy's friends, as well as each of our family members, would commemorate the gentle closing of this door behind us and the blazing of a new trail that was being laid out in front of us.

One by one, the various items were gathered and ready to be delivered by yours truly. I was fully packed and ready to hit the road as soon as I finished this task of love and appreciation. Andy's friends could have easily chosen to stay sad and then quietly move on with their lives, but they chose instead to stay in the thick of everything, right there with me and the rest of my family.

The wakeboard and life-vest that Andy dearly loved was given to his best friend Bryce, with whom he had shared so much time out on Bartlett Lake. They were both kindred souls who were fearless and loved pushing the envelope with each other whenever they could. The depth of love these two boys had for each other was profound and no doubt will last another lifetime through Bryce.

Andy's favorite maple bat that he had moaned so longingly over and that we finally bought went to another of his best friends, Degan. These two not only shared their great love of baseball, but they also shared the true adventure of the sport, such as good and bad coaches, inclement weather, heartbreaking losses, and also exuberant wins.

I gave Blaze a special shadow box with Andy's favorite baseball jersey proudly displayed inside. The summer before Andy moved, they had both played on the Los Angeles Dodgers Scout Team, which made for such fond memories for everyone—especially Blaze.

I remember a time we followed behind Blaze in my SUV, as we drove to California to play in a big tournament. I thought to myself, "Wow, that kid drives fast and crazy!" Blaze is one of those special souls who still calls me every Mother's Day to wish me a happy day. Blaze is a sensitive guy and has always been so incredibly thoughtful. I love that young man so very much. He reminds me so much of what I know Andy would be like if he were still living with us.

Colton had a knack for finding a bit of trouble and adventure just about everywhere he went. I gave him a framed picture as a fun reminder of the time he and Andy had gotten stuck pretty deep in the mud with Colton's jeep. This was just one of the many wacky times the two of them shared, as Colton was also one of Andy's closest and dearest friends. As a reminder, it was Colton's mom Karen who lovingly prepared all the photo boards and videos for Andy's memorial service.

Noah's gift was a framed picture taken the morning of their first day of freshman year in high school. From the time they were in second grade, Noah had also been one of Andy's very best friends. They had gone to the same schools from kindergarten up and shared the same birthday month, which they usually celebrated with a sleepover. Starting with little league, Noah was on the same baseball team as Andy, followed by the same teams in grade school, club teams, and finally varsity baseball—quite an amazing feat since they were just freshmen that first year they played.

I will always remember the trip home from San Diego, when they were both sitting contentedly in the back seat of our truck. Noah is of Asian descent, so he was proudly—but not necessarily so successfully—teaching Andy to sing Jap Rap. It was one of the funniest things I have ever witnessed.

A huge bag of sunflower seeds went to David, who had been the varsity baseball team manager. Although David has Down syndrome, he has never let that stop him from anything. He has a passion for baseball every bit as much as all the other boys, and Andy always held such a special place for David in his heart. David would continue to be a big part of everything we did with the foundation, and he never forgets to mention his friend Andy, who, as David so loves to say, is now pitching no-hitters in Heaven.

A favorite jersey and framed picture of their band of brothers went to Tristen, who had also been one of Andy's most treasured friends from the time they were very small. The amazing foursome—Noah, Tristen, Colton, and Andy—made a very tight-knit little group, and it was a bond that would last through high school.

Even though Tristen went to a different school, it didn't lessen the bond these four boys had with each other. They all lived in the same neighborhood and would often be found spending the night at each other's homes, eating everything in sight as they grew into robust teenagers.

Jared became one of Andy's closest friends, too, over the years. The two of them shared a close spiritual journey. Jared also lived in the neighborhood, and after Andy's move, would become a part of the band of brothers listed above. Andy and Jared would go to winter and summer church camp together every year, as well as church on Sundays and Wednesdays. There is such a sweet picture of the two of them under a tree at church taken the Easter before Andy moved. Since they had shared such a strong bond of faith, I think Andy's suicide was particularly hard on Jared.

Each of his great friends would no doubt ask the questions—either out loud or to themselves—What is it that I missed? Why didn't I know? Could I have somehow stopped him if I had known? All very haunting questions, considering the closeness of all of their relationships.

Last but not least, Katie—the love of my Andy's life. I'm certain the loss of Andy will remain one of the most difficult things this young woman will ever have to face in her life. While they were no longer boyfriend and girlfriend at the very end, it never changed the depth of what they shared—from starting out as best friends when they were little to developing into what was a true first love for both of them. Though they were just sixteen when Andy moved, the bond of love the two of them shared was as extraordinary as it was deep.

Jared, Katie and Andy were drawn even closer together by their deep faith and love for the Lord, which they shared since they were all in sixth grade. Going to church camps together over the years continued to strengthen and solidify their bond. Thankfully, I have many a fun, goofy video these kids made together while just messing around, usually over at Katie's house. Katie, too, had a mama that could really cook—and for any growing teenage boy, that's always a huge plus.

It was with Katie, out on Bartlett Lake, that Andy had videotaped my famous outing—or upping, shall I say—on the wakeboard. I'm so happy to know that Andy got to experience a love with someone as precious as Katie. I gave some of Andy's ashes to Katie, as well as his church sweatshirt, and a framed picture of the two of them taken in Mexico, sitting on the rooftop of a house they were working on for a local family.

Through a project sponsored by our church, Katie and Andy had gone down there together as volunteers to work on a building project at a local orphanage. Oh, how I wish they were still up on top of that roof. They looked so young and so incredibly beautiful. In that moment that's forever frozen in time, their whole lives lay ahead of them, just waiting for them to grab hold.

Fortunately, we can't ever see what lies ahead, which allows us to live in each precious moment and savor all that life has to offer us.

To each present I attached a handwritten card detailing the great appreciation that I had for their friendship—with Andy first, and with me. I probably could have survived the last eighteen months on my own, with just my biological family, but it was much easier with all these great kids in my life—and for that I will always be grateful.

After all was said and done, and each of the gifts had been delivered and opened, I packed up my truck—Andy's truck—and headed up the long road to North Dakota. Though I felt some joy in all of the giving, each of my visits had been excruciatingly painful and had completely drained me of all reserves. I would need this time, on the drive out to see Clay, to replenish my soul and piece back together my broken heart. I had planned on spending the next two months with Clay, where I could be free from so many reminders back home of our missing link. The one who completed our family circle. Our Sunshine.

As I ventured toward a new beginning, I was reminded of a saying that my beloved grandmother and mother would both often say to me. I carried the tradition forward, using it on my kids over and over again, as they were growing up.

I would say to them, "Bloom where you are planted." It was echoing in my memory banks again, on this day, and I realized this might be something I would need to do again, just as I had done so many times in years past.

Our lives had forever changed, and I was now heading up to a town where I didn't know a soul except Clay—and didn't know what I was going to do with myself once I arrived. While I knew I was in dire need of good rest, I also knew that too much free time might prove to be detrimental.

After some nurturing from my dear husband and some treasured books, I, too, would have to figure out how to rebuild my life, at least for the summer months ahead.

Two days later, I arrived at Clay's temporary home. After some much-needed downtime, I headed out one morning for the local nursery to buy something symbolic of breathing fresh life back into my heart. Life had significantly changed and it didn't look anything at all like I had anticipated. So, I purchased a beautiful blooming rose bush to take back home with me to plant, and I would begin the process of finding new life for myself.

On my way home, something caught my eye and I felt a stir deep in my soul. The offices of the local newspaper, located in between the nursery and our apartment, were calling to me quite loudly.

My truck seemed to veer itself into the parking lot. Once I had parked, I boldly marched into the office of the newspaper's editor in chief. Much to my amazement, he agreed to see me—and, I'll confess, I nearly shocked myself when

I heard myself asking him to allow me to write a weekly column for the paper. Now, this is not something that I had ever done before, and yet I felt called to do this. He asked me what my column would be titled and asked me to send him a sample of my first week's musings.

I drove home, smiling in silent reflection. After potting my brand-new rose bush, I began writing my first-ever weekly column for The Dickinson Press, aptly titled, "Bloom Where You Are Planted."

Just wait until you see all that has blossomed and grown out of that amazing summer I spent healing in North Dakota.

Dylan

3-6-02 ~ 4-11-18

About the Author

LeAnn Hull was born and raised in Phoenix, Arizona and has been married for 39 years. While raising their four children, she and her husband, Clay, owned and operated a construction company, Arizona Window Center. Being self-employed allowed LeAnn the time to invest in their children's lives and in the community in which they lived.

As a member of the business community, it was necessary to be involved with the local business chapters and continuing education organizations in order to provide the customer with the most up-to-date product information. These groups continued to expand LeAnn's horizons and desires. This eventually led her to run for a seat in the United States Congress in 2010.

Never at a loss for words, this opportunity provided a platform to voice her desires for a greater business community and better fiscal responsibility in our country. After many campaign speeches and debates, it became evident that speaking was one of LeAnn's gifts and passions. Having the ability to make a difference in people's lives through inspiration and motivation was extremely satisfying.

KASH JACKSON REED

July 12, 2002 – February 27, 2018

Kash. 2008

About Andy Hull's Sunshine Foundation

Andy Hull's Sunshine Foundation was created in 2013 to raise awareness of suicide prevention while providing skills to deal with life's challenges.

Within months of her son Andy's transition, LeAnn Hull established Andy Hull's Sunshine Foundation, inspired by her son's nickname, with the goal of sparing even just one person the pain and anguish of suicide. Impacting many children, teens and adults, the Foundation talks about coping skills, triggers, and tools to use during difficult times, all with a "You Matter" approach.

The Foundation has sparked a worldwide movement with their yellow "YOU MATTER" wristbands. To date, over 200,000 wristbands have been distributed, at no cost. With suicide rates rising, the wristbands are a tangible reminder of the foundation's important message.

For more information, visit *www.andyssunshine.com*.

In Support of LeAnn Hull

When the construction company I work for invited LeAnn Hull to address the personnel on our site in East Texas with a topic of Mental Health on the Job. it piqued my interest. While most large companies are insured for job-related mental health issues, the topic itself is rarely, if ever, discussed. When LeAnn spoke about the long-term effects of the job (being away from family, difficult feelings and depression), it was an impassioned, heart-driven message to which our workers paid close attention. As a result of LeAnn's talk, our crew learned that it's okay to recognize there is a problem and that it's also okay to seek help when needed. Although LeAnn's drive for this work was born out of her own personal tragedy, she has turned her message into a powerful tool for reaching members of the construction community (and many others) in order to do everything that she can to prevent more unnecessary tragedy in our world. Her words are a gift for all of us – from LeAnn and also from Andy.

Mark Kennedy
Site HSE Manager
Linde Engineering North America
Houston, TX

This compelling book is part family journey and part "how-to" survival kit for those dealing with the death of a loved one by suicide. LeAnn Hull takes the wisdom she has personally shared with hundreds of thousands of people worldwide, and provides the detailed backstory here, in these pages. LeAnn illustrates by personal example, a number of highly effective coping skills. In so doing, she shows us how to also rise up out of the depths of despair and find a life of purpose and hope.

- Suzanne Giesemann
Evidential medium and author of
Messages of Hope and *Still Right Here*
Hilton Head, SC

Featuring LeAnn Hull as our guest speaker during "I Matter" week at our school (April 2019) was the highlight of the entire event. Her testimony of using the loss of her son to empower the lives of others resonated with not only the students, but also the staff. Watching LeAnn's pain be transformed into what has quickly become her purpose was a timely blessing that I hope will linger with every student she encountered as they continue to experience life's many celebrations and challenges. As a parent and educator, I can only hope that the lives of my child and students will be positively impacted by something I've said or a connection I've helped them make. LeAnn Hull is that true life-changing connection for all of us.

Tuere Dunton-Forbes
Professional School Counselor
Charlotte, NC

I first met LeAnn in 2010, when I was an Arizona State Senator and she was running for U.S. Congress. I was the moderator of a debate among Congressional candidates and was immediately impressed with LeAnn and her brilliant demeanor. My daughter had met LeAnn a few months earlier and they had quickly become very close friends. This strong woman was running for Congress for all the right reasons – most importantly, to make a difference in people's lives. LeAnn has made a significant difference in people's lives; though, as it turned out, not in the way she had first envisioned. The combination of strength and compassion in LeAnn that I saw during the 2010 debate would prove to be a great asset in the years ahead when LeAnn had to cope with the unfathomable tragedy of losing her beloved 16-year-old son Andy by suicide.

There has been a significant increase in teenage suicides. Although the reasons are all different, the outcomes are always the same. LeAnn knew that teachers and other school personnel had to be trained to see that whenever a child's behavior radically changes, it is a warning sign that can't be ignored. Teachers are on the front lines with these kids every day, so alerting and working with their parents can indeed mean the difference between life and death. Sadly, it's too late for Andy, but LeAnn is determined to ensure that other families will not have to suffer as hers has.

LeAnn wanted to provide training for school personnel, and I volunteered to help. Good training already existed, but there needed to be a way to get it into all the schools statewide. Given my experience as a (former) State Senator, I had the expertise and connections to help make it happen. LeAnn and the Andy Hull's Sunshine Foundation that she co-founded worked tirelessly to educate Arizona legislators. Legislation was introduced in 2014 to mandate the much-needed training, but for complicated reasons, the bill was altered – so it only allowed for Suicide Prevention and Awareness Training to count as Continuing Education Credits. The bill successfully passed, and many teachers were trained, though not enough. The 2019 legislative session finally mandated this life-saving training for educators and all other school personnel throughout the State of Arizona. LeAnn accomplished her goal to make a difference in people's lives and will continue to make a significant difference for many more years to come.

Senator Barbara Leff
Arizona Senate, 11th District
2003-2011

I was twenty-two years old and two months pregnant with my first child when I received the horrific call that my father had committed suicide. I went through all the emotions of guilt, anger, grief and pain that were beyond comprehension. I wonder how my life might have been different if a book like *How to Live When You Want to Die* had been available to me during that time. LeAnn met one of the toughest challenges in her life when she heard these words about her beloved son Andy, "He's dead." Feeling that death by suicide is far too common, this courageous woman turned her pain into power and created Andy Hull's Sunshine Foundation. *How to Live When You Want to Die* is a life-changing gift to the world. It helps promote healing among those who have grieved suicide and also offers help to those who might be contemplating. In this book, LeAnn shares various coping tools that she used to survive. I highly recommend *How to Live* and strongly believe that it should be used as a survival handbook in every home.

Debra Martin, evidential medium, healer and
author of five books; most recently, Proof of Miracles

LeAnn's devotion to saving lives by educating students and teachers about suicide awareness and prevention is the most unselfish, emotionally exhausting work imaginable.

Even more impressive, what LeAnn does outside of speaking publicly and running her foundation is truly life giving. She is actively engaged in saving the lives of other mothers struggling to survive the loss of a child to suicide. I am one of those moms. I spent over a year attending meetings for families who have lost a child or lost a loved one by suicide, but without finding any true lifeline. I'm sure it was divine intervention that had LeAnn at one of these meetings.

There is something in the eyes of a mother who has lost a child by suicide that made me instantly recognizable to LeAnn – and she reached out to me. When I heard her share her story in vivid detail, for the first time since the loss of our son Christopher, I knew someone else knew and understood my pain. LeAnn had not only survived but had thrived – and she made her heart open to me. For the first time in well over a year, I felt hopeful.

After her presentation, LeAnn and I spoke of our spiritual lives and our beautiful, brilliant, athletic sons. We spoke of our "normal" families. We spoke of our pain, rage and dysfunction. And we spoke the word SUICIDE. Out loud.

From that day forward, I have known – through LeAnn's example – that it is the responsibility of each and every person to be present to those at risk, to be educated, and to be comforting to those experiencing the unending devastation of a child lost way too soon to suicide. Thank you, LeAnn, for opening my eyes and also for reawakening my heart.

Anne Park
Phoenix, AZ

Shortly after Andy moved to heaven, LeAnn and I went with our dear friend Craig and LeAnn's mom Mary to lunch, in the hopes of spending quality time together after some of the chaos had passed. While there, all four of us agreed wholeheartedly to embark on a life-changing journey. Together, we took a leap of faith and put our new vision for hope and healing into God's hands. This was the seed out of which Andy Hull's Sunshine Foundation first grew, and from that day on we have been dedicated to educating others and saving lives. LeAnn Hull is the strongest women I know. Although she can't change the past, she is certainly changing the future – one talk and one "You Matter" bracelet at a time.

Carolyn Leff
Scottsdale, AZ

You never really think how much your life can change in an instant – until it does. In December 2012, LeAnn had asked me to do her a favor. Her husband Clay would be coming home soon for Christmas and she wanted the house to be especially clean when he arrived. I went to LeAnn's house to let the cleaning crew in on her behalf. That's when I found Andy's lifeless body lying on the floor. In that instant everything changed – and life has never been the same for anyone. Four months after Andy's death, I helped LeAnn form Andy Hull's Sunshine Foundation. Over the past six years,

I have watched it become a lifesaver – not only for those families we serve, but for LeAnn, her family, and me. Suicide not only affects the immediate family, but also everyone surrounding them. LeAnn and I have a death bond that I don't believe anyone will ever quite understand. I still get triggered sometimes, but I seek help whenever that happens and push through it. *How to Live When You Want to Die* was written from a place of great pain and also tremendous strength. Reading this book and implementing the tools reflected herein will be a terrific start on the path of your own healing journey.

Craig Dean
Phoenix, AZ

We can't always control what happens to us in life; but we can, to some extent, control our responses. While most people run away from the grief and tragedy of others, LeAnn Hull runs toward it. She is an extraordinary first responder for those in the aftermath of loss to suicide who are freshly experiencing the horror and trauma of their darkest grief. In 2012, within the first few hours of her own unimaginable horror, LeAnn looked into the eyes and hearts of all the kids and families filling her home and recognized their need for hope. She saw written on their faces the thought that *if this amazing, happy and talented kid could die by suicide, might it be an option for me, too?* LeAnn knew that those young, vulnerable friends of Andy "Sunshine" Hull needed to hear a message of truth and also that they are important. They needed to hear that no matter what comes their way, the answer is *never* suicide. And they needed to know that they matter to someone.

Like a phoenix rising up from the ashes, the overriding message born out of LeAnn's tragedy was "You Matter!" In the days, weeks and months after Andy's passing, while wracked with agonizing grief, LeAnn was propelled forward through the aftershock in a seemingly supernatural way.

LeAnn is a gifted inspirational speaker, a successful busi-nesswoman and former candidate for Congress who is also a mother of four and grandmother of three. She pressed into her gifts, talents and experience, and funneled her grief into a purpose she never imagined would be hers to fulfill - form-ing Andy Hull's Sunshine Foundation.

LeAnn first introduced the message of "YOU MATTER!" during an assembly of a grieving and confused student body where Andy had attended high school and was so revered. So powerful and profound was her message that a long line of young people waited to hug LeAnn after her talk and to express their own feelings of hopelessness and thoughts of suicide. It was undeniable to LeAnn that changes needed to be made in our schools, communities, places of worship, military and beyond. She realized we needed to talk about suicide and mental health as freely as we talk about drugs, alcohol and safe sex.

In her relentless pursuit of change, LeAnn has taken her message of "YOU MATTER!" all over the country and abroad, giving countless speeches, presentations and work-shops in schools, military bases, and businesses. LeAnn has fought hard for change in school districts, imploring admin-istrators to talk about suicide and to provide students with resources for coping with today's challenges.

As a result of the foundation's efforts, Arizona House Bill 2605 was signed into legislation in 2014, allowing Suicide Awareness and Prevention Training to be counted as con-tinuing education credits for teachers and administrators. The powerful yellow "YOU MATTER!" wristbands that LeAnn hands out wherever she goes have crossed interna-tional borders; a message that has had far reaching ripple ef-fects of hope.

LeAnn has said that losing a child to suicide is not a club you ever want to join. She's right. Having learned to live with her loss, she shares insights into grief, breaks down barriers to healing, and corrects harmful words and actions that are casually thrown around in well-meaning attempts to bring comfort.

Since that very first assembly, LeAnn has been a champion for change, inspiring others to see value in themselves. To believe our lives have a purpose only we can fulfill. To live when you feel like dying. Let LeAnn's life after loss inspire you. Let the words in this book bring you courage and hope. And may you believe each and every day of your life that you are valuable – and You Matter!

Laura Mesenbrink
Katie's Mom
Phoenix, AZ

Nathan's Flower Arrangement   10-31-84 to 04-26-2014